JUMPS
PHILOSOPH
CLASSR

This collection of inspiring and simple-to-use activities will jumpstart students' understanding of philosophy, and is a treasure trove of ideas for building philosophical enquiry into the curriculum. It offers teachers a range of quick, easy and effective ways for developing children's comprehension of and engagement with philosophy, and will help them 'learn how to learn'.

With a wealth of activities, including puzzles, class discussion techniques and group tasks, *Jumpstart! Philosophy in the Classroom* covers the following topics:

- curiosity and imagination
- language for thinking
- critical thinking
- creating a community of enquiry.

Practical and immersive methods will encourage children to think, analyse, evaluate, discuss, judge and arrive at reasoned conclusions across all areas of the curriculum, stimulating philosophical conversation and changing the way that content is processed and understood in the classroom. This book will be a vital resource for all those who want to develop thinking skills and philosophical enquiry in their school.

Steve Bowkett is a former teacher and author of numerous books for teachers including the bestselling *Jumpstart! Creativity*. He visits schools to run creative writing workshops for children and also works as an educational consultant specialising in the areas of thinking skills and problem solving, creativity and literacy.

Jumpstart!

For a full list of titles in this series, visit
https://www.routledge.com/Jumpstart/book-series/JUMP

Jumpstart! Philosophy in the Classroom
Games and activities for ages 7–14
Steve Bowkett

Jumpstart! RE
Games and activities for ages 7–12
Imran Mogra

Jumpstart! Study Skills
Games and activities for active learning, ages 7–12
John Foster

Jumpstart! Wellbeing
Games and activities for ages 7–14
Steve Bowkett and Kevin Hogston

Jumpstart! Apps
Creative learning, games and activities for ages 7–11
Natalia Kucirkova, Jon Audain and Liz Chamberlain

Jumpstart! Grammar (2nd Edition)
Games and activities for ages 6–14
Pie Corbett and Julia Strong

Jumpstart! Talk for Learning
Games and activities for ages 7–12
John Foster and Lyn Dawes

Jumpstart! PSHE
Games and activities for ages 7–13
John Foster

Jumpstart! History
Engaging activities for ages 7–12
Sarah Whitehouse and Karen Vickers-Hulse

Jumpstart! Geography
Engaging activities for ages 7–12
Sarah Whitehouse and Mark Jones

Jumpstart! Thinking Skills and Problem Solving
Games and activities for ages 7–14
Steve Bowkett

Jumpstart! Maths (2nd Edition)
Maths activities and games for ages 5–14
John Taylor

Jumpstart! Spanish and Italian
Engaging activities for ages 7–12
Catherine Watts and Hilary Phillips

Jumpstart! French and German
Engaging activities for ages 7–12
Catherine Watts and Hilary Phillips

Jumpstart! Drama
Games and activities for ages 5–11
Teresa Cremin, Roger McDonald, Emma Goff and Louise Blakemore

Jumpstart! Science
Games and activities for ages 5–11
Rosemary Feasey

JUMPSTART! PHILOSOPHY IN THE CLASSROOM

GAMES AND ACTIVITIES FOR AGES 7–14

Steve Bowkett

LONDON AND NEW YORK

First published 2018
by Routledge
2 Park Square, Milton Park, Abingdon, Oxon OX14 4RN

and by Routledge
711 Third Avenue, New York, NY 10017

Routledge is an imprint of the Taylor & Francis Group, an informa business

© 2018 Steve Bowkett

The right of Steve Bowkett to be identified as author of this work has been asserted by him in accordance with sections 77 and 78 of the Copyright, Designs and Patents Act 1988.

All rights reserved. No part of this book may be reprinted or reproduced or utilised in any form or by any electronic, mechanical, or other means, now known or hereafter invented, including photocopying and recording, or in any information storage or retrieval system, without permission in writing from the publishers.

Trademark notice: Product or corporate names may be trademarks or registered trademarks, and are used only for identification and explanation without intent to infringe.

British Library Cataloguing in Publication Data
A catalogue record for this book is available from the British Library

Library of Congress Cataloging in Publication Data
A catalog record for this book has been requested

ISBN: 978-1-138-30985-2 (hbk)
ISBN: 978-1-138-30987-6 (pbk)
ISBN: 978-1-315-14354-5 (ebk)

Typeset in Palatino and Scala Sans
by Saxon Graphics Ltd, Derby

 Printed in the United Kingdom
by Henry Ling Limited

In Remembrance of Harrison Ballantyne, whose death aged 11 challenges all philosophies

Contents

Acknowledgement   x
Introduction   xi

1   Jumpstart curiosity and imagination   1
       'What could this be?' game   2
       Question cascade   3
       So what is philosophy?   4
       Being nosy   5
       The simile game   6
       Mind warm-ups   7
       Opinions   8
       Codes   9
       Creative cut-ups   9
       Join the dots   10
       New inventions   12
       Really listening   14
       Paris is the capital of France   15
       New words and combinations   16
       Category cards   16
       A hierarchy of understandings   17
       Thought experiments   19
       Visualising   20
       Philosophical thought experiments   20
       Strength of reasons   24
       The Ship of Theseus   25
       End of the world   26
       Telling you something true   26
       The ladder to the moon   28
       Question hunt   30
       Big ideas   34
       Moments of change   35
       What's worth knowing?   36

2 Jumpstart language for thinking　38
   Creating a healthy language environment 39
   Definitions 41
   Synonyms 43
   What's in a name? 43
   Nominalisation 46
   Sombunall 47
   Precise questioning 48
   Pluralising 48
   Metaphors again 48
   Analogies 49
   Truth is like ... because 53
   Snap judgements 54
   Perspectives 55
   Chinese whispers 57
   In your own words 58
   Subtle differences 59
   What's the point? 62
   Rhetoric 63
   Phil and Sophy 64

3 Jumpstart critical thinking　72
   4 Cs thinking 72
   Look carefully and think 73
   Give me an example of ... 74
   Working with concepts 75
   Would you rather ... 77
   A matter of opinion 79
   A sample argument: violence in videogames 83
   Infoscraps 84
   Five pressures that can inhibit children from
      taking part in class discussions 93
   Oversimplification 96
   Abstractions 99
   Ambiguity 104
   Shift of meaning 107
   Surface structure and deep structure 108
   Criteria of quality in a philosophical enquiry 111
   Kinds of questions 116

Dialogue revisited   119
So what is a philosophical question?   124
Embedded assumptions   124
Contradictions   126
Moral dilemmas   128

4   Jumpstart a community of enquiry   131
Personal preparation   131
Setting up the space   132
Getting ready to think   133
Stimulus   134
Thinking time   134
Question making   138
Airing and sharing the questions   140
Choosing which question to discuss   141
First thoughts   142
Building: the core of the enquiry   142
Last thoughts   143
Review   144
The role of the facilitator   145
Skills checklist   145
Sample dialogue   147
Afterword   152

Notes   154

References   155

Acknowledgement

Grateful thanks as ever to my friend Tony Hitchman for his artistic talents and to Sue Dixon for giving me the opportunity to delve more deeply into philosophy in the classroom.

Introduction

The word philosophy comes to us from the Greek 'philosophia' meaning 'a love of wisdom', though the term also implies a desire for knowledge and an active pursuit of meaning; and by 'love' we mean taking pleasure from these activities and a firm intention to know more and seek further, deeper meanings. 'Wisdom' can be traced back to the Old English 'wis', linked to 'wit/wits', with its connotations of being 'learned, sagacious, cunning; sane; prudent, discreet; experienced; having the power of discerning and judging rightly' (Online Etymological Dictionary). So while knowledge and wisdom are complementary, they do not amount to the same thing. Lao-tzu, the person (or persons) who wrote the philosophical/religious text the *Tao te Ching* (*c.* 550 BCE) asserted that 'He who has extensive knowledge is not a wise man' – though I would want to modify that by saying, 'He who has extensive knowledge is not *necessarily* a wise man', and of course by substituting 'person' for 'man'.

While many might think of philosophy as being the highly complex and abstract pursuit of academics (which it often is), the evolution of philosophy in schools (the P4C – Philosophy for Children – movement mentioned below) follows the Socratic method of enquiry, after the Greek philosopher Socrates (born *c.* 470 BC). This is a form of collaborative dialogue where viewpoints are shared and explored based on asking and answering questions coupled with the use of critical thinking to attempt to reach the truth – or at least some degree of consensus about the matter in question. Such a method is *dialectical*; using discussion and systematic questioning to construct reasoned arguments. The word *argument* here is not used in the everyday sense of a quarrel, nor does it carry the suggestion that the outcome should be about winning or losing.

In philosophical enquiries all participants are valued equally and are seen as co-creators of fresh perspectives and deeper understandings. As such there is no attempt to persuade fellow enquirers to adopt a particular point of view through rhetorical or emotive language, position of authority, or through charisma or any other 'force of personality'. Similarly, while someone may feel strongly about the particular subject under consideration, emotional outbursts are discouraged and the greatest respect is shown to all those taking part in the discussion.

The guiding principles of philosophical enquiry then, as far as Socrates was concerned, are that true knowledge is sought not taught – though we might pause to reflect on what 'true' means here – and that the focus and outcomes of exploration of meaning feed back to the individual in a practical way, in the form of insights and guidance on how we can best live our lives. Socrates is credited for having said, 'The unexamined life is not worth living', seeing philosophical enquiry as a pragmatic pursuit bringing benefits to everyone.

In short, P4C as it is practised in schools:

- Celebrates and respects the ideas and viewpoints of individuals, and is inclusive rather than exclusive or elitist.
- Uses 'communities of enquiry' to help individuals explore and clarify their values and beliefs, and to evaluate the worth of these.
- Makes use of systematic questioning and reasoned argument as the driving forces towards uncovering deeper understandings.
- Is intended to be of practical value in helping people live more fruitful and fulfilling lives.

As far as we know, Socrates believed that the choices we make are largely motivated by the desire to find happiness. He felt that the wisdom of an individual depends upon the degree to which they know themselves, which in turn is linked to their ability to reason. Someone who can reason clearly and incisively is more able to make choices that would result in increased happiness based on a consideration of values, beliefs and possible courses of action.

Introduction

The P4C 'movement' originated in the USA in the 1960s with the development of resources by Professor Matthew Lipman and his associates at Montclair University. Lipman believed that children can think in an abstract way from an early age and that teaching them reasoning skills would not only empower their thinking but help them to become more 'reasonable' – able to reason – in making decisions and interacting with others. Like the philosophers of Ancient Greece, Lipman saw that the ability to think effectively led to 'practical wisdom' in the form of good judgement, and that this should be the primary goal of education.

Since Professor Lipman's pioneering work the P4C movement has grown considerably and become international. In Britain the Society for Advancing Philosophical Enquiry and Reflection in Education (SAPERE)[1] – which is also the Latin word for 'I am wise' – The Philosophy Foundation[2] and Philosophy for Schools[3] – are just a few of the organisations offering resources and training for schools wishing to embed philosophical enquiry in the curriculum. And that's an important point. A 'P4C school' doesn't regard enquiry sessions as a mere add-on, as something to be slotted in when time allows, but rather as a vital feature of the school's ethos, practised within the wider context of policies and programmes for thinking that underpin the whole approach to teaching and learning across the curriculum.

As we have already seen, children forming communities of enquiry are encouraged to listen carefully to and respect others' viewpoints while confidently expressing their own thoughts and feelings. Supported by the teacher (though facilitator is the preferred term), children's thinking is thus valued, which leads to greater self-confidence and heightened self-esteem; these being boosted further by children's evolving ability to write and speak more articulately.

Various government pronouncements about children's learning reflect the aims of thinking skills/P4C programmes in schools.

> [The curriculum] should equip [pupils] with the essential learning skills of literacy, numeracy, and information and communication technology, and promote an enquiring mind

and capacity to think rationally. The school curriculum should contribute to the development of pupils' sense of identity through knowledge and understanding of the spiritual, moral, social and cultural heritages of Britain's diverse society and of the local, national, European, Commonwealth and global dimensions of their lives. It should encourage pupils to appreciate human aspirations and achievements in aesthetic, scientific, technological and social fields, and prompt a personal response to a range of experiences and ideas.

The school curriculum should promote pupils' spiritual, moral, social and cultural development and, in particular, develop principles for distinguishing between right and wrong. It should develop their knowledge, understanding and appreciation of their own and different beliefs and cultures, and how these influence individuals and societies. The school curriculum should pass on enduring values, develop pupils' integrity and autonomy and help them to be responsible and caring citizens capable of contributing to the development of a just society.[4]

Personal, learning and thinking skills (PLTS) provide a framework for describing the qualities and skills needed for success in learning and life. The PLTS framework has been developed and refined over a number of years in consultation with employers, parents, schools, students and the wider public.

The framework comprises six groups of skills:

- independent enquirers
- creative thinkers
- reflective learners
- team workers
- self-managers
- effective participants.

Functional skills should be integrated into the curriculum. To be effective, functional skills teaching must be relevant and allow learners to engage with real situations in the real world.

Learners need opportunities to:

- apply their skills in plausible contexts or use their skills for real purposes
- engage with the world beyond the classroom
- integrate learning by linking knowledge within and between the functional areas
- spend time planning and developing their work
- make choices and decisions, think creatively and act independently
- experience success in real situations as a result of using their skills effectively.[5]

The document goes on to list functional skills in different subject areas. Here are some examples.

ENGLISH

- Communicate information clearly and succinctly in speech and writing.
- Express a point of view reasonably and persuasively.
- Read and understand information and instructions, then use this understanding to act appropriately.
- Analyse how ideas and information are presented, evaluating their usefulness, for example in solving a problem.
- Make an oral presentation or write a report.
- Contribute to discussions and use speech to work collaboratively to agree actions and conclusions.

MATHEMATICS

- Possess the analytical and reasoning skills needed to draw conclusions, justify how these conclusions are reached and identify errors or inconsistencies.

CITIZENSHIP

- Discuss the issue (speaking and listening).
- Find out all relevant viewpoints (reading/Internet/book/newspaper research).
- Consider solutions and any alternatives (discussion/problem solving).
- Write a report or summary of the issue.
- Write a letter of concern or support to your local MP.[6]

All of the above supports Albert Einstein's famous assertion that 'we cannot solve our problems with the same thinking we used to create them'.

HOW TO USE THIS BOOK

Like other titles in the Jumpstart series, this book is intended to be a practical resource full of activities and techniques that you can implement quickly and easily, and across a wide age and ability range. Also in line with other Jumpstart books, this one seeks to point the way towards further sources of information and help should you wish to go down the path of becoming a thinking/P4C school. (Having said that, if you are already such a school, then hopefully you will still find plenty of useful ideas here!)

Many of the activities may be used as stand-alone activities or combined in different ways to fit in with your own teaching-and-learning agenda – these are cross-referenced as necessary. In addition, to facilitate the 'dip-in' feature of the book, some activities appear in more than one section, although read in conjunction with each other they will offer more than looking at just one of them.

The overall aim of *Jumpstart! Philosophy in the Classroom* however is to show you how to establish a self-supporting community of enquiry and to run P4C sessions of increasing richness and depth. As such, some ideas and skills necessarily need to be introduced before others and this will be indicated in the text.

Finally, to paraphrase the author and critic Christopher Hitchens, it's worth taking the risk of thinking for yourself, as it leads to greater happiness, truth, beauty and wisdom. That in a nutshell is the baseline justification for doing P4C.

A NOTE ON THE TEXT

Usually the text addresses you, the teacher, directly. Occasionally paragraphs are written as though addressed to the children. These are simply my suggested ways of framing questions and tasks when you set them for the class.

CHAPTER 1
Jumpstart curiosity and imagination

Children are naturally curious, creative and imaginative. In his book *A Whack on the Side of the Head: How You Can Be More Creative*, author Roger von Oech recounts how, when he was a sophomore (mid-teens) in high school, his English teacher drew a chalk dot on the blackboard and asked the class what it was. After several seconds had passed, someone said, "It's a chalk dot on the blackboard." Everyone seemed relieved that the obvious had been stated. When no further ideas were forthcoming the teacher expressed her surprise and mentioned that when she had done the same activity recently with a group of 5-year-olds they had come up with around 50 different ideas.

An ancient Chinese proverb tells us, 'In the beginner's mind there are many possibilities but in the expert's mind there are few'. An important function of education is to celebrate and cultivate the uninhibited creative energy that young children so often display while adding to their repertoire of thinking skills such that the ideas they have can be explored, analysed, reflected upon and refined with increasing sophistication. Or as Roger von Oech says, 'Every child is an artist. The problem is how to remain an artist after growing up.' Showing children how to 'do philosophy' is a practical and enjoyable way of achieving this, You can start children off as soon as they begin school, as teacher Sara Stanley demonstrates in her book *But Why*, explaining that by the time they reach Year 3 most of the young philosophers are capable of discussing abstract concepts in depth (see the If-Then game on page 80 for an example of this).

Incidentally, the 'chalk dot game' is a great way to jumpstart children's imaginations at the start of any lesson where you want them to actively engage with the ideas you present. Vary the activity over time by using dots of different colours and a variety of shapes such as those in Figure 1.1. Either choose an image deliberately or use dice rolls to select a shape randomly.

'WHAT COULD THIS BE?' GAME

Prime the children's thinking by asking, 'What could this be? What does it remind you of?' Running this activity from time to time will boost children's creative ability and their self-confidence in expressing ideas. At the outset the typical response to shape 3/3 will be 'a star'. Later and more original ideas may include 'a laser beam bouncing off mirrors', 'a five-sided box with the top flaps unfolded', 'a five-petalled flower', or 'an optical illusion – two glass arrowheads laid one on top of the other'.

When I play this game during school visits, once all the ideas are in I say, 'And out of all of those answers you've given me, which is the right answer?' Almost invariably one or more children will say, 'any of them' or 'all of them', to which I reply, 'That's very wise'. Then I ask that out of all the ideas I've heard, which is the best idea? Most youngsters have got the message by now and chorus, 'any of them' or 'all of them'. to which I reply, 'That's very wise'.

Figure 1.1

Take it further
Explain these two important principles of thinking creatively.

1. To have our best ideas we need to have lots of ideas.
2. How many ideas can we have and what use can we make of them?

In discussing these principles with the class, point out that 'best' is what I call a slippery word – that is to say, a word that carries a particular meaning in my mind but may have different meanings in the minds of the people I'm talking to. Ask for adjectives other than best to describe ideas. Further point out that the second principle necessitates two different kinds of thinking. Generating ideas effectively requires children to be in 'brainstorming mode', allowing thoughts to pop up without conscious effort – say it as you think it: the chalk dot game is a clear example of this. Making best use of children's suggestions (whatever you decide 'best' might mean here) requires deliberate analytical/critical thinking and a more systematic exploration of the ideas.

QUESTION CASCADE

Choose one of the words used to ask open questions – who, what, where, when, why or how – place it in the middle of a display board and invite children to write their question suggestions on sticky notes to place around it. To begin with, emphasise that children don't have to know the answers in order to ask the questions. In subsequent lessons, work with the children to categorise some or all of the questions, including those that potentially have a right answer but one which cannot be discovered (Exactly how many people are alive in the world right now?), and those that may be inherently unanswerable (Is the universe infinite?) (see also page 154 note 18).

You may well find, as I have done, that many children delight in asking big questions that often form the basis of philosophical enquiries. Most recently this happened when I was running a writing workshop with a group of Year 6 children who, so their teacher told me, had 'learning challenges'. We were aiming to write science fiction stories and were talking about robots, spaceships, planets and aliens when Jaydon wondered in all seriousness, 'Yes, but why do we have stars? Why is the universe made of stars rather than something else? Why is the universe here at all?' The temptation to talk about these things rather than write stories was almost overwhelming – but we had to get the writing done! Incidentally, Jaydon's question echoes that of the German philosopher Gottfried Wilhelm Leibniz (1646–1716) who asserted that 'The first question which should rightly be asked is why is there something rather than nothing?' Contemporary philosopher Steven Law suggests that this is perhaps the greatest mystery of all and discusses it in his book *The Philosophy Files 2*.

SO WHAT IS PHILOSOPHY?

When you first ask the class this question you're likely to get references to the Harry Potter stories. Quite a number of children also believe that philosophy has something to do with the stars (which on thinking back to Jaydon's questions it has). Other definitions I've encountered from children include:

- Philosophy is talking about things you can't measure.
- It's trying to understand other people's thoughts.
- It's using your imagination to think about impossible things.
- It's about wondering why.
- Philosophy is about looking deeper into words.
- It's playing with ideas to see where they can go.

And, I have to say, my favourite:

- Philosophy is talking about ideas that are too big to fit inside one person's head.

It's interesting to collect children's definitions before you've established a community of enquiry. As these examples show, some are very insightful. Once your class becomes familiar with philosophical thinking ask the children to define philosophy again to see how far their understanding has developed. (Some time ago I was invited to a school to run some thinking skills workshops. I happened to say to one boy in my first session, 'So I understand you do philosophy at this school?' To which he replied, 'Well it depends what you mean by "philosophy" and "do" and "school".' Which both answered my question and properly put me in my place.)

It's also worth asking, as you 'do' 'philosophy' at 'school' with your class, what skills or attributes they think are useful when taking part in an enquiry. Children's responses may simply echo what you've already told them, but again some ideas are perspicacious. The following answers are from Year 5 and 6 pupils:

- You've got to really listen and think.
- You can change your mind and no one criticises you for it.
- You can have your own opinions but must make them stronger with reasons.
- You should stick to the point.
- You can disagree with people but must always respect them.
- You must be patient waiting for your turn and not interrupt.
- You must be confident to ask what people mean sometimes.
- You must try and see things from other people's point of view.
- You can feel OK even if you haven't got any answer at the end (of an enquiry).
- You've got to be nosy and want to find out more.

This last point resonates with what I often tell children about thinking creatively, that two important ways of 'being nosy' are noticing and asking questions, or we might say displaying awareness and curiosity. These are key behaviours which support the development of other thinking skills, and lay the foundations for meaty and meaningful philosophical enquiries.

BEING NOSY

Some years ago while working with Sara Stanley on the 'But Why' project I wrote a picture book called *Philosophy Bear and the Big Sky*.

Philosophy Bear himself was invented by Sara, while I dreamed up Pinkerton the very nosy cat and Story Owl, who almost always answers a question by telling a story, often leaving you wondering what the story had to do with the question you asked (though in time the penny will drop as you have one of those lovely Aha! moments). Pinkerton loves to try and notice at least ten differences between, for example, two leaves or shells, two coins or spot-the-difference visuals (easily found online). This is a useful challenge to set the children. Split the class into pairs and give each pair examples of the above and ask the children to notice as many differences as possible.

Take it further
Show the class two almost identical pieces of writing. Explain that there are (however many) differences in punctuation, spelling and word choice, and ask, can the children find them all?

Present the class with two words or phrases that are similar in meaning and ask what the difference might be. Is being reasonable the same as being fair? How is rage different from anger? (Notice the embedded assumption that it is.) Is being brave the same as being fearless? (On this point, see the sample dialogue on page 147.)

Just as Pinkerton loves to be nosy, so Philosophy Bear loves to ask questions of different kinds. Ask the class to come up with questions that:

- Have one right answer.
- Have more than one right answer.
- Have a right answer but we can never find out what it is.
- May have no answer at all.

THE SIMILE GAME

Take a big idea such as life, freedom, identity, happiness, etc. and hitch it up to some similes. At first, offer the complete comparison but then invite the children to suggest ideas.

- Life is like a rollercoaster because it has its ups and downs, but if you have the right attitude it's an exciting ride.
- Life is like a story because it has a beginning, a middle and an end. Also because there are heroes, villains, problems and journeys.
- Life is like a tasty dinner because the ingredients go together and are to be savoured.
- Life is like a forest because?
- Life is like a song because?
- Life is like a school because?
- Life is like a … because?

And so on.

If you are working with a concept like happiness, be sure to keep children to the point. You are not looking for examples of what *makes* someone happy – happiness is three scoops of ice-cream covered in sprinkles – but rather comparisons that show some depth and insight.

Incidentally, you can use the same technique to help children understand how potentially powerful their minds are and the different kinds of thinking they can do.

- Your mind is like a horse because?
- Your mind is like a rocket because?
- Your mind is like a classroom because?
- Your mind is like a spider's web because?

MIND WARM-UPS

While a philosophical enquiry relies on reflection and analysis of words and concepts (i.e. careful critical thinking), it also requires creativity and imagination. For example, during one enquiry a Year 6 class was exploring the notion of courage. One pupil offered the familiar notion that 'courage is doing what you fear to do'. Another child then asked, 'So what if a soldier in battle could swallow a pill that would take away all of his fear – would he still be courageous by doing what he no longer feared?' (See also the sample dialogue on page 147.)

A what-if like this is not just an imaginative idea; it digs deeper into the core theme of the discussion by testing the concept of courage. Generating such ideas depends on a certain 'lightness of mind', a degree of faith in one's own creative abilities and an attitude of playfulness. As such, beginning an enquiry session with a 'mind warm-up' spins children's thinking up to speed and helps put them in the mood to thoroughly explore the topic in question.

We've looked at a few games of this kind, but here are some more that may appeal.

OPINIONS

Pick a topic where different people have different opinions. For example, children should not be made to come to school, but should be able to decide for themselves.

Help the children to write out as many ideas as they can, first agreeing with the idea, then disagreeing with it. Write each idea on a separate scrap of paper.

Scramble up the scraps.

- Now ask the children to separate out for and against ideas.
- Now separate out facts from opinions.
- You now have four piles of ideas – for, against, fact, opinion. Ask the children to pick out what they think are the most persuasive opinions and the facts that most strongly support the case (for or against).

Take it further
Look in the letter pages of newspapers or have-your-say posts linked to online news items to find lots of topics that you can use for the above activity.(See also the 'Infoscraps' activity on page 83.)

Learning benefits
- Develops reasoning abilities.
- Helps children to question facts.
- Encourages balanced exploration of arguments.

CODES

Help the children to make up some codes so that they can write secret messages to each other and to friends. Here are a few basic ideas, but you will find plenty more on the Internet.

- Turn letters into numbers. The most obvious is to make A1, B2, C3, etc., with Z as 26. Or do it the other way around, with A as 26 and Z as 1. Play with other combinations to make the code harder to crack.
- Make one letter stand for another. Z could stand for A, Y could stand for B, etc.
- A variation on this is to jump a certain number of letters ahead in the alphabet to make your code. So if you jumped, say, three letters ahead, A would become D, B would become E and so on. Or you could simply scramble the alphabet so that each letter is coded by another, random, letter.
- Make a 'shape code'. In the same way that Morse Code uses dots and dashes for letters, use squares and triangles (or any other shape that's quick and easy to draw).

Learning benefits
- Develops concentration and logical thinking.
- Creates the opportunity to discuss the alphabet – where letters come from, how they have developed, etc.

CREATIVE CUT-UPS

Create a sequence of objects that are arranged in a logical order, scramble them and then ask the children to re-create the sequence. So a simple version of the game would be to put the following in order of size:

- Moth – elephant – sparrow – cat – goat – whale – monkey.

A more complicated sequence would be:

- The planet Neptune lies beyond Uranus.
- Mercury circles the sun inside the orbit of Earth.
- Neptune is the eighth planet of the solar system.
- Pluto lies outside Neptune's orbit.
- Venus orbits the sun between Mercury and Earth.
- Mars is next outward from the sun after the Earth.
- Jupiter and Saturn both orbit the sun closer-in than Uranus does.
- Jupiter orbits the sun further out than Mars.
- Saturn is the seventh planet outward from the sun.
- Mercury orbits closest to the sun.
- Jupiter's orbit lies after Mars and before Saturn.

Learning benefits
- Encourages research.
- Develops logical thinking.

JOIN THE DOTS

Give each child or group a sheet of random dots. Pick a topic such as animals, machines, geometrical shapes, monsters, etc. and ask the children to join dots to create their outlines.

Take it further
This is a good opportunity to explain that for thousands of years people have pictured animals, monsters, gods and heroes made from the stars in the sky. This is how we come to have constellations ('gatherings of stars'). There are many books that tell the stories behind the constellations. Read these to your class and then ask the children to make up different myths and legends to explain the actual constellations or the ones they have created on their sheet of dots. (See also 'Ladder to the moon' (Figure 1.6).)

Learning benefits
- Introduces or develops knowledge of myths and legends.
- Boosts the imagination.

Figure 1.2

NEW INVENTIONS

Make two lists, each featuring six objects from around the house. Roll dice to pick an item randomly from each list. The aim of the game is to have ideas for handy new inventions.

1.	soap	light
2.	book	table
3.	TV	hot water bottle
4.	shoes	coat hanger
5.	chair	electric socket
6.	cup	shampoo

Figure 1.3

Tip: This game works best if you 'brainstorm' ideas, simply saying what comes to mind without thinking about whether the ideas are silly, useful, etc.

For example:

- 4–6 shoes/shampoo – shoes with compartments for shampoo, toothpaste and either useful toiletries just in case you need them.
- 6–3 cup/hot water bottle – a double hot water bottle. One compartment contains hot water, the other tea, coffee, etc. so that you can pour yourself a hot drink before warming your feet.
- 5–6 chair/coat hanger – a chair with a hook on the back where you can hang your jacket.

Take it further
Make a 6×6 grid, and fill in the boxes with words and pictures so that you have more options for creating new inventions. You can also theme your grids – for example, Communications, Learning, the Environment, Transport and so on.

Learning benefits
- Promotes creative thinking.
- Gives practice in brainstorming.
- Three feet underground: visual word puzzles

In this activity, how you position the words gives a clue to a well-known phrase or saying. See Figure 1.4 for an example.

<u>**GROUND**</u>
FEET, FEET, FEET

Figure 1.4

We have the word 'feet' appearing three times under the word 'ground', and that's how the game works. Figure 1.5 gives some more examples.

1. W
   WORD
      R
       D

2. GIVE-GET, GIVE-GET, GIVE-GET, GIVE-GET

3. GOOD all TIME

4. MUCH, MUCHMUCH

5. YOU just ME

6. NE ???

7. <u>TERM</u>
      2

8. TIM

9.   C
   LEVEL

10. *MEAT*

Figure 1.5

Answers:

1. Crossword
2. Forgive and forget (four 'give' and four 'get')
3. All in good time ('all' in between 'good' and 'time')
4. Much too much
5, Just between you and me
6. Any questions
7. Half term
8. Tiny Tim
9. Below sea level (below 'C', 'level')
10. Lean meat (I know, this is the corniest of them all!)

Learning benefits
Encourages lateral thinking/interpretation of visual clues.

REALLY LISTENING

Ask the children to become still and relaxed and simply listen to the sounds going on around them. It helps if they close their eyes so that they're not distracted.

Afterwards, ask the class some questions about what they heard, such as:

- What was the nearest sound you heard?
- Which was the farthest sound?
- Which sound went on the longest?
- Were there any sounds you couldn't identify?
- What was the sound you liked most?

Take it further
Use household objects to make sounds one at a time. Ask the children to describe them. You can suggest vocabulary such as soft, harsh, high-pitched, whispery, etc.

Find a suitable picture and ask the class to imagine what sounds would be there.

Learning benefits
- Develops listening skills (auditory acuity).
- Encourages descriptive language.
- Develops metacognition (noticing and controlling one's own thoughts).

PARIS IS THE CAPITAL OF FRANCE

Give the children a fact such as 'Paris is the capital of France' and encourage them to explore and analyse it by reflecting on some of the following questions:

- Why do you think it is? (speculating)
- What does it mean for a place to be called a capital? (recalling, inferring)
- What does a place need to include for it to become a capital? (researching)
- Can a town or a village become a capital? (speculating, linking pieces of information)
- Who decides which place becomes the capital of a country? (speculating, researching)
- How would life change if the place where you live became a capital? (speculating, inferring)

Take it further
Pick one or two of the questions from the list that you didn't talk about in class and write down your replies/answers at home.

It is a fact that London is the capital of England. How do we know that something is a fact? Can something that is not true be a fact? Can you find any examples of things which were facts once but are not any longer?

What is an opinion? Are some people's opinions 'better' than others'? How do you think an opinion can be made to have a greater influence than before? Write down three facts and three opinions about London.

Learning benefits
- Develops a range of thinking skills.
- Encourages critical questioning.
- Creates an opportunity for research.

NEW WORDS AND COMBINATIONS

Prepare a list of prefixes and attach them to the names of everyday objects. What new gadgets come to mind? For example, anti (against) as in anti-gravity, anti-junkmail letterbox, anti-steam glass, anti-cold-caller telephone. Auto (self) as in autobiography, autoshower, autobed, autobook. Meta (change) as in metamorphosis, metahome, metamobile, metapet, metapod nano.

What new collective nouns might we attach to; people talking together on their mobile phones/fallen leaves/homework books/ children who've just come in muddied-up from play/shoppers queuing two days early for the January sales/people who own a pink Ipod nano?

What groups might these new collective nouns refer to: an apathy of/a zing of/a pointedness of/a skiffle of/an attainment of/an illusion of?

Learning benefits
- Increases vocabulary.
- Encourages creativity and imagination.

CATEGORY CARDS

Create a set of category cards (e.g. mammal, bird, fish, etc.) and a set of 'parts' cards, any of which may apply to one or more of the categories (has wings, can swim, is warm blooded, lays eggs, etc.).

Lay out the selection of category cards face up on the table, then shuffle and deal the parts cards. The children can look at their own hand of parts cards. The first child to play lays down one parts card (e.g. has wings). If the next child has a parts card that may be added to the first card because they can both apply to the same category (e.g. lays eggs), then she can play that card. At this stage the parts cards may refer to birds or insects. The third child plays another parts card (if he has one) that will add to the category. If he wants to play safe he can also select a category card, place it on top of the pile and win that pile for himself. However, he may choose not to do that if he thinks he can win a bigger pile of parts cards at his next turn – though he runs the risk of another player winning the category with a smaller pile of cards in the meantime.

Learning benefits
- Revision of knowledge.
- Creative linking.

A HIERARCHY OF UNDERSTANDINGS

Professor Kieran Egan of Simon Fraser University suggests that as children grow they come to understand the world in different ways, displaying a range of what he calls 'cognitive tools': somatic, mythic, romantic, philosophic and ironic. The first four mirror the characteristics and timing of Jean Piaget's stages of cognitive development: sensorimotor, pre-operational, concrete operational and formal operational.

Somatic ('of the body') understanding occurs from birth until around the age of 2. Here children learn a variety of physical activities, usually by copying the behaviour of others, and develop a non-verbal appreciation of the world. Mythic understanding (ages 3 to 7) is reflected in the development of language and thinking in terms of binary opposites – more subtle gradations occur later – metaphors and stereotypes. Mastery of this form of understanding is helped by socialising the child into the myths of the culture. Here, 'myth' is defined as a story that recounts the early history of a people or that explains natural and social phenomena, often through the agency of supernatural characters and events. While myths are not literally true, they help young children to develop a shared sense of right and wrong. (See 'Telling you something true' on page 26.)

Romantic understanding occurs from around 8 to 14 years. The main goal here is the mastery of literacy. This kind of understanding is also characterised by an ongoing sense of wonder coupled with an idealised (romantic) view of reality but also the need to uncover limits and extremes of human potential.

Philosophic understanding unfolds from around the age of 15 into adulthood, and signals a person's growing ability to understand the world in terms of theoretical abstractions. In other words, we develop a framework of ideas about how the world works based on earlier experiences and information. One drawback of this stage of development is that one's framework of understanding can become rigid and less amenable to change (what has been called a 'hardening of the categories'). We can become set in our ways of seeing unless we are prepared to reflect on our values and beliefs, and to modify them if they are found wanting. Ironic understanding can achieve this. This mode of thinking is characterised by the ability to reflect in a more sophisticated way coupled with a degree of scepticism; a willingness to question ideas and beliefs etc., rather than an uncritical acceptance of 'theories' about how the world works.

The ages at which these different modes of understanding appear are generalisations. My belief is that cultivating philosophical thinking in children can accelerate their progress through the hierarchy of understandings while at the same time enriching the way a child understands the world at any given stage. As we have seen, educators such as Sara Stanley teach children as young as 5 to 'do' philosophy, often using myths, fairy-tales and other stories to show values and beliefs in action and to explore the nature and consequences of moral dilemmas. Running philosophical enquiries also feeds older children's 'romantic' view of the world – big questions such as 'Is there a God?' 'Where did the universe come from?' 'How do I know what is real?' and so on nourish a sense of wonder while helping satisfy the need to explore and define limits and boundaries. Philosophy in the classroom also paves the way for the development of the 'world theories' that are a feature of philosophic understanding, yet also encourages children to engage in the kind of reflectiveness characteristic of the ironic understanding that prevents a framework from becoming a cage (see Egan 1997).

THOUGHT EXPERIMENTS

A thought experiment uses the imagination to devise, explore and test hypotheses, either where the experiment may not be possible in the real world or to predict potential outcomes of experiments that are possible.

One of the most famous thought experiments was created by Albert Einstein when he was just 16 years old. He wondered what the universe would look like if he could travel at the speed of light and imagined himself zooming along at the same velocity as a light beam. He reasoned that this would allow him to view the light beam as though it was frozen in space as 'an electromagnetic field at rest though spatially oscillating'. Such an act of imagination led Einstein to decide that 'everything would have to happen according to the same laws as for an observer who, relative to the Earth, was at rest'. No one is certain whether or not this is the case, but Einstein's daydream planted the seed that led to the great theoretical leap which developed into his theories of relativity.

Another such envisioning supposedly came from Galileo and is known as his 'Leaning Tower of Pisa experiment.' Here, two metal balls of different masses were dropped simultaneously from the Leaning Tower of Pisa. Earlier, Aristotle had reasoned that objects will fall at a speed relative to their masses, in which case the more massive ball would land first. Galileo's theory of gravity predicted that, in the absence of air resistance, objects of different masses would fall at the same rate. Some commentators tell us that Galileo actually performed the experiment, while others believe that it was just an act of imagination. Whatever the truth, Apollo 15 astronaut David Scott carried out the experiment on the airless lunar surface in 1971, dropping a feather and a hammer from chest height. Both fell at the same speed and landed together, thus proving that Galileo's theory was correct.

VISUALISING

Visualising is an important and potentially powerful way of thinking that has useful applications in philosophy. As a precursor to what follows, take the class through some guided visualisations, making them longer and more involved over time. This will help children internalise their awareness more effectively and increase their concentration span.

A simple instruction such as 'imagine you are a seagull' is all that is needed initially. Notice how many of the children adopt a look of concentration immediately. Prompt and guide as necessary to sustain and enrich the visualisation – imagine you are flying over a funfair at the seaside. Land on the rollercoaster and enjoy the ride. When it stops, fly away over some sand-dunes. It's a sunny day, but after a while the sky clouds over and it begins to rain. Find a hole in a cliff overlooking the sea and, sheltered and warm, watch a storm develop; noticing the changing shades of the clouds, flashes of lightning and the boom and rumble of thunder … .

You can prepare guided visualisations beforehand or make them up as you go along. Invite the children to come up with their own examples and lead their classmates in these adventures of the imagination.

Tip: Visualising may also be used to help children relax and serves as a precursor to meditation and mindfulness work (see *Jumpstart! Wellbeing* in the References and Resources section). Putting yourself in someone else's shoes in the imagination also helps develop empathy and gain insight into other people's point of view.

PHILOSOPHICAL THOUGHT EXPERIMENTS

Imagined scenarios are used extensively in philosophical enquiries to explore concepts and to try and resolve moral dilemmas. Here are a few: you can find plenty more online.

One of the best known is called the trolley problem. Ask the children to imagine that an evil villain has tied five of his enemies to the railway track. A trolley or train is speeding down the line out of control and will soon kill these five people. Luckily you are standing right by the points and can pull the lever to divert the train. However, the villain has tied his greatest enemy to this other line.

So, the big question is: Do you pull the lever to divert the train?

Encourage the children to support their decisions with reasons. Sometimes children will ask questions before making a decision. For example, 'Are the people tied to the railway lines evil?' You might respond by asking in return if that would make a difference. You can also make the most of the thought experiment by positing variations on the basic scenario:

- The five people tied to the line are strangers to you but the lone person on the other line is your friend.
- The five people are evil but the lone person is innocent and good (and vice versa).
- One of the carriage doors on the train is hanging open. If you pull the lever it will hit you – you won't have time to get away – so that you will either be paralysed for life or killed. Does that fact alter your decision?
- The five people are elderly and near the end of their lives. The lone person is a child.
- It's your much-loved pet that is tied to the second line. Does that fact influence your decision?

Imagine that you did not know there was a lone person tied to the second line. You pull the lever and the person is killed by the speeding train. Does that make you guilty of murder? Would you be more guilty if you pulled the lever knowing there was a lone person tied to the second line? How do you define guilt?

The trolley problem was devised by the British philosopher Philippa Foot, much of whose work was in the field of ethics. It is a dilemma (from the Greek 'twice' and 'premise', or 'double proposition') because either choice is undesirable. One function of this dilemma is to question a major theory of ethical philosophy, which argues that the most moral decision provides the greatest good or happiness for the greatest number (this is the basic tenet of Utilitarianism). Pulling the lever would sacrifice one person to save five. Critics of this standpoint argue that making the decision is still clearly immoral, while another point of view asserts that because you are part of the event you are *compelled* to act; that doing nothing would be equally if not more immoral than pulling the lever.

Take it further
Explain utilitarianism to the class. Ask the children how far they agree with the principle of the greatest happiness for the greatest number, then help them to test it by offering different dilemmas. Sometimes these can be based on 'real life' situations you find in the news. The following is an example.

You are the head of a committee that must decide whether or not to allow an oil company to set up a fracking plant in the middle of an area of outstanding natural beauty. Giving permission would mean destroying part of an ancient woodland plus the construction of a road passing very close to a nearby scenic village. This would result in a dramatic drop in house prices in that village. In addition, the increased traffic to and from the plant would cause pollution levels to rise, which might affect the health of local people. However, building the plant would create dozens of new jobs and bring a great deal of money to the area.

*

The county council is struggling to maintain services because of a reduction in government funding and will be forced to close one of the following: a local youth club, a job centre, a social club for pensioners, a crèche, a local branch of the Citizens Advice Bureau, the local library.

Which would you vote to close down and why? Put them in the order in which you would close them if money became even tighter:

put your choice of the first to close at the top of the list and the last you'd close at the bottom. Why did you choose this order of closure?

However, all of these establishments can remain open if council tax is increased by 5 per cent. Would you vote for this option instead? What if the council tax increase had to be 10 per cent? At what percentage increase would you say no to tax rises and begin closing these local services?

Tip: If some children don't relate to this dilemma because they are not taxpayers, tell them that the cash needed would have to come out of their pocket-money and/or savings – i.e. make it personal! This reinforces a common phenomenon in philosophical discussion; that while the issue at hand may stir up strong emotions because it touches upon one's values and beliefs (moral, political, etc.), points still need to be made in a reasoned and reasonable way, showing all due respect to others who may hold very different views.

*

After leaving a supermarket with your groceries you discover that you have been under-charged by £10. Coincidentally you had intended to donate the same amount to a local charity that helped your best friend through a serious illness. You know that the charity is struggling for money, but you also know that the supermarket cashier's mistake means that that person will receive £10 less in their pay packet when the cash register is tallied up.

- Do you return to the supermarket and offer the £10 back to the cashier?
- Do you go to the charity shop and give them the £10?
- Do you go to the charity shop and give them the £10 plus the £10 of yours that you were going to donate anyway?

Now change the scenario. You find that you have simply been undercharged £10 at the supermarket and had no intention of donating to charity. Would that alter what you did with the money? What if you had made a bigger purchase somewhere else and had been undercharged by £50 – would that influence your decision about what to do with the money?

STRENGTH OF REASONS

Supporting a viewpoint with sound reasons is important in philosophical enquiry. Some reasons are stronger (more morally defensible or backed by evidence and facts) or more acceptable than others. Here are six reasons why you might not go back to the supermarket. Note that you're not being asked whether you agree with any of these reasons, but simply to assess their strength in terms of how acceptable or convincing they are.

1. It's your mother's birthday and the £10 will buy her a nice present.
2, The cashier probably wouldn't say anything if you had been *over*charged £10, so why should you say anything now?
3. You don't discover that you're £10 better off until you get home, which is over a mile from the supermarket. You can't be bothered to walk back there and then home again.
4. Your pet cat needs a life-saving operation and the £10 will help towards that.
5. The supermarket chain makes millions of pounds of profit every year, so won't miss a measly £10. But £10 is quite a lot of money to you.
6. On your way home you come across a homeless person and give him or her the £10, thus justifying not returning to the supermarket.

Now put these reasons in order of their 'strengths'; that is, how acceptable or convincing you find them to be. Put the strongest reason first. Note that you don't need make a strict 1–6 list, as you may find two or more reasons to be equally strong (or weak).

Can you think of any other reasons why you wouldn't report the £10 undercharge to the supermarket? If so, where would you put them in your list?

Jumpstart curiosity and imagination

Considering your strongest reason, does that reason make keeping the £10 the 'right' thing to do?

There are more moral dilemmas on page 105. If you are working through this book sequentially, the children will have been introduced to more ideas and skills by the time you reach them, thus ensuring a meatier discussion.

*

THE SHIP OF THESEUS

This is a paradox rather than a moral dilemma (a paradox being a person or situation combining contradictory features or qualities, or a statement that at first seems absurd but which may nevertheless be true). It is one of the oldest thought experiments, coming to us through the writings of the Greek essayist Plutarch.

Imagine a ship that has been kept seaworthy for 100 years owing to constant repairs and replacement of worn parts. Now not a single piece of the original ship remains. Is it the same Ship of Theseus when the craft was launched? If not, when did it stop being so – when 51 per cent of the parts were replaced, or some other percentage?

The philosopher Thomas Hobbes added something to the problem. If you took all of the old parts of the ship that had been removed and used them to build a new vessel, then which of the ships would be the real Ship of Theseus? Or would they both be?

Variation: If it's true that most of the cells in the human body are replaced every seven years or so, am I the same person now as I was when I was a baby?[7]

END OF THE WORLD

The world is about to be destroyed by a giant asteroid. A spaceship has been built to carry 12 people to Mars, where they can build a new colony. Who do you think should be granted a place on the spaceship and why? Note that you do not have to name particular people – you might just include 'a doctor', 'an engineer', etc.

TELLING YOU SOMETHING TRUE

Two monks were walking back to the monastery in the hills after buying food at the market. On the way they came to a ford, the bed of which was littered with sharp stones. On the nearside a woman was wondering how she could get across without ruining her sandals or hurting her feet and soaking the hem of her long skirt, as she was carrying two bags full of vegetables and fruit.

The younger monk immediately introduced himself and offered to carry the woman across, then return for her bags of food. She accepted gratefully. After she was safely on the other side of the ford the monks went on their way.

The elder monk was very angry about what his companion had done, because one of the rules of the monastery was that the monks should never talk to any woman. He managed to keep his anger to himself until they were almost home, then expressed his outrage at the younger monk's actions, giving him a stern reprimand.

The young monk listened calmly and then said, 'I put the woman down on the far side of the ford, but I see that you've carried her all the way back to the monastery' (Reps 1980).

This story is really about 'putting down your anger' or 'not carrying your disapproval beyond the event'. It is an example of a (presumably fictional) tale that 'tells you something true'; an analogy, a parable. Use this and others – you can find plenty online – to get children thinking about fiction and fact.

The Concise Oxford Dictionary (fifth edition) offers one definition of fact as 'a thing certainly known to have occurred or be true' and tells us that fiction is 'feigning, invention, a thing feigned (invented) or imagined; a conventionally accepted falsehood'. In my experience this is what most if not all children believe – that fiction is something made up and not true, while a fact is something discovered and true.

Earlier we looked at thought experiments from science (page 19) which led to the discovery of new facts about the world or the universe. In other words, imagined scenarios – 'fictions' like Einstein moving alongside a light beam – helped uncover matters of fact. Similarly, philosophical thought experiments may be fictional insofar as they never happened, or never could happen, but nevertheless form the basis of enquiries that can move us nearer to 'truths' about the world, including human values, beliefs and actions.

Interestingly, one online dictionary defines true as 'in accordance with fact or reality' and offers synonyms that include accurate, correct, verifiable, faithful, literal. Meaty enquiries can be based on questions such as 'what is truth?' and 'what is reality?', and as a preparation for these you might (at any point in the children's development as philosophers) ask them to think about the following.

a) I have an astronomy book that is a few years old and it says that Saturn has 60 moons. I have another astronomy book from the same year and it says that Saturn has 60 *known* moons. At the time of writing (January 2017) one website[8] says that 'Saturn has 62 confirmed moons'.

- Are all of these statements examples of facts?
- Are all of these statements equally true?
- Can we say that one fact may be less true than another?

(To its credit, the coolcosmos website also says, 'More moons are constantly being discovered so check the NASA Saturn site for the latest.')

b) Is the story about the two monks factual? Is the story about the two monks true? Does the story tell you something true?
c) 'I was really resentful that my rival got the job and I did not. When I came home my wife said, "Well you've got a chip on your shoulder!"' Is what my wife said true, and in what sense?
d) Can something that is not a fact be true? What examples can you think of?
e) I watched a factual TV documentary yesterday about an abandoned kitten and that upset me. Today I read a short story about an abandoned kitten that upset me just as much. If my upset today was based on fiction, was it less real than my upset based on a factual documentary?
f) Can fiction be 'real' in any way?
g) What does it mean to believe something? Can we in any sense believe something that is fictional? What examples come to mind?
h) Is there a difference between believing something and believing *in* something?[9]

THE LADDER TO THE MOON

This beautiful metaphor originally referred to an idea from the oral storytelling traditions of Africa. The ladder links everyday anecdotes and gossip ('earthy tales') to the great creation myths which seek to explore and explain (not literally perhaps) big questions such as where did the universe come from?; why does it exist?; what is my purpose in life? – the same questions that form the basis of rich philosophical enquiries.

For our purposes the idea of a ladder that links the ordinary with the numinous (spiritual and immeasurable) and the universal may be used in several ways.

- It serves as a visual reminder of the Socratic principle that philosophy is a means of seeking a richer and happier life for all people. It is not and should not be the exclusive pursuit of academics.

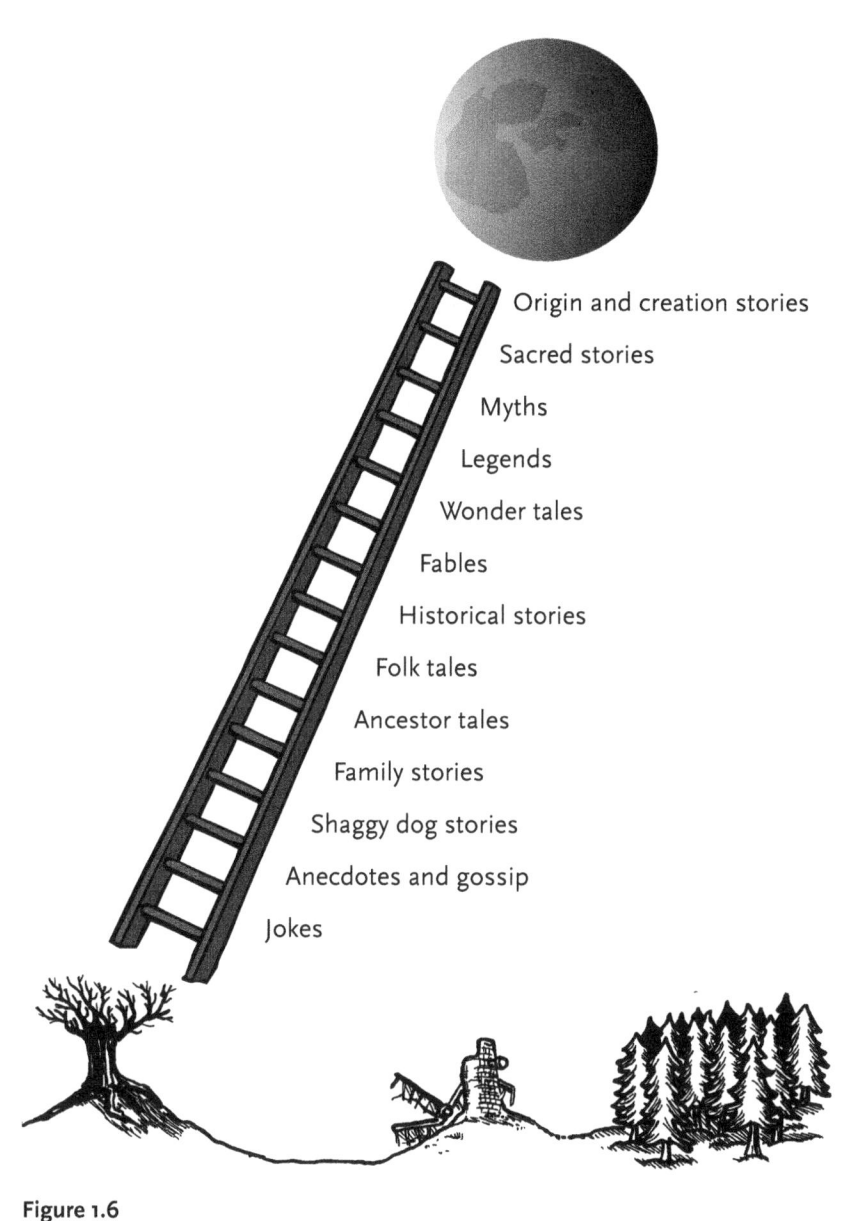

Origin and creation stories
Sacred stories
Myths
Legends
Wonder tales
Fables
Historical stories
Folk tales
Ancestor tales
Family stories
Shaggy dog stories
Anecdotes and gossip
Jokes

Figure 1.6
Source: Tony Hitchman

- There is a 'direct line' between our day-to-day experiences and the most profound questions that we can ask.
- Fables, wonder tales, legends and myths are often stories that 'tell us something true'. Whether or not some stories of this kind were thought to be literal explanations of natural phenomena, for example, they may be read as figurative explorations of 'real life' themes such as good and evil, morality, freedom, justice, identity, purpose and others. The common definition of a myth, for instance, as 'a widely held but false belief or idea' is naïve in that it perpetuates the juvenile view that 'stories are made up and are not true'. The mythologist Joseph Campbell felt that the symbols of mythology are all around us, woven into the fabric of our daily lives, and that they offer guidance as to our conduct for bringing the greatest benefits to ourselves and to others (Campbell 1991, 1994). Similarly, the work of the psychologist Carl Jung links mythical themes and imagery to archetypal (basic, subconscious) instinctive forces of the human psyche.
- Stories are vehicles for a range of philosophies; explorations of life's important themes, the consequences of our actions and the nature of morality. Looking at the world mythically (metaphysically) is different from looking at the world scientifically, but both ways of seeing are necessary and fruitful, and both may be incorporated into the search for wisdom and truth, which the practice of philosophy aims to facilitate.
- Tales of all kinds may be used as a stimulus for a philosophical enquiry, but myths and legends especially are rich sources of ideas that can easily be made accessible to children in the form of textual versions, films and comics.

Note: Typing 'ladder to the moon' into a search engine brings up a variety of references that have no connection with the way the phrase is being used here. Be discerning.

QUESTION HUNT

Various studies have found that questions asked in classrooms about lesson content are often initiated by the teacher rather than by the pupils; that many of these questions refer to answers that the teacher already knows and merely require recall of previously delivered information. Many of the questions asked by pupils are 'procedural', which is to say they are about the 'mechanics' of the lesson – Shall we do this in our best books? Are we to finish this for homework? Can I sharpen my pencil? (see e.g. Morgan and Saxton 1994). Keying 'questioning in schools' will bring up further references plus links to sources of advice on encouraging children to ask more effective and incisive questions, which will very quickly improve their understanding of the information you are giving them, and which paves the way for them to become more capable philosophers.

A quick and easy activity to improve the variety and quality of questions you want the children to ask is the 'question hunt'. Here you present the class with a portion of a comic book or extract from a story and invite the children to ask questions about it. Leave it at that for now, making clear that neither the children nor you are expected to know the answers. The purpose of the activity is to begin to shift the children's behaviour away from taking part only if they think they know the answers, while cultivating greater self-confidence because there is no hidden agenda to the activity – you just want to gather their questions. In preparing for the session I tell children that the word 'question' and the word 'quest' come from the same root, 'to search'.

So, referring back to the story of the two monks (page 26), one Y5 class came up with the following questions:

- Why was it a rule that the monks should not talk to women?
- Is a rule the same as a law?
- Why did the young monk break the rule – was it just to help the lady? What other reasons might there be for his actions?
- If the older monk had helped the woman and so broken the rule, would he be setting a good example to the younger monk or a bad example? Why so?
- What if the woman was being ambushed by bandits as she stood by the ford – would the older monk have broken the rule too I wonder? Would he have been wrong to do so?

- When is it OK to break rules? (Typing 'rules are made to be broken' into a search engine brings up plenty of links that will help open out this issue.)
- What punishment if any should the young monk receive for breaking the rules?
- If the young monk had helped a man cross the ford, does that make the rule sexist?
- If the monks had found a baby girl abandoned by the ford, would it be breaking the rule to take her to safety somewhere? Would the older monk have broken the rule, do you think? Why so?
- What has not talking to women got to do with believing in God?
- If God is good and kind, why is there a rule which says you cannot help a woman? And who might have made up the rule: God, the monks at the monastery, or someone else?
- What reasons could God have for making up a rule like that?
- How does the rule help the monks learn more about God and serving God?
- What other rules from the monastery could help the monks learn more about God?

Take it further

Help the children to work out what different kinds of questions are being asked here, linking these to various thinking skills such as speculating, inferring, reasoning, interpreting, etc., and which rely on opinions and/or on facts that can be researched. Keep the children focused – point out that the task is not to discuss personal beliefs about whether God exists or not (that would form the basis of a future enquiry).

What questions can the children now come up with about this little scenario (Figure 1.7)?

Figure 1.7
Source: Tony Hitchman

BIG IDEAS

Philosophical enquiries are often based on big ideas such as reality, good versus evil, knowledge, truth, freedom, power, purpose, belief, identity, life and death. As they stand they are vague, overarching concepts: the purpose of philosophy is to explore them, 'unpack' them and relate them usefully to one's everyday life and conduct.

A first step (which we will develop in later chapters of this book) is to take one of these key concepts and make an association web around it. Place the big idea in the middle of a display space, hand out sticky notes and encourage the children to link it with whatever comes to mind: questions, anecdotes, simple word links and so on. As with the question hunt activity (page 30), the focus is not about debating the issue or knowing the answers to any of the questions, but to begin to add detail to the concept; to create a rich field of ideas that can form the basis of future enquiries.

One Year 6 class I worked with chose 'identity'. Some of the children's additions were as follows:

- Where does the word identity come from?
- I heard about this person who has a split personality. Does he have more than one identity?
- Do I have an identity when I'm asleep?
- Would an intelligent computer have an identity?
- Do animals have identities?
- Have you got to be able to think to have an identity?
- Identity is who I think I am.

Identity theft
- If I was cloned, would my clone have the same identity as me?
- The things I own are about me, but they are not *me*. [And from the same child] I know who I am, but it's hard to explain to others.
- Do new-born babies have identities?
- If a person is loved and remembered when he has died, does he still have an identity?

Take it further
Take two of the big ideas and ask the children to generate questions that link them. Thus, for example, good-evil + freedom:

- If there is a God, why are people allowed to be evil?
- Should murderers ever be set free from prison?
- Can an evil person ever choose to become good?
- Are some people born evil?
- Is it ever right to do something evil?
- Is it ever right to do something bad (if you think bad has a different meaning from evil)?
- If I'm sleepwalking and I commit a crime without knowing what I'm doing, am I as evil as I would be by committing the same crime when I am awake?

MOMENTS OF CHANGE

Ask the children to reflect on ideas and experiences that have changed their perspective or way of thinking. Encourage the recollection of pleasant and positive experiences but do not prevent children from talking or writing about negative experiences if they feel they need to. This activity can be a useful lead-in to 'what's worth knowing?' below. You might consider offering some examples of your own: here are a few of my life-changing moments, if you'll indulge me.

When I was about 10 years old some friends and I camped out on the hills above our town. We were lying out on the grass on a warm summer night when Nigel Lloyd noticed a moving light in the sky. He asked the rest of us what it was and I said it was a star that had broken loose from its orbit and was drifting away through the universe. That was nonsense of course and I knew it, but my friends took me at my word. I decided to try to find out what we'd seen (it was a particularly bright artificial satellite) and that led to a lifelong interest in astronomy and in science more broadly.

When I was 13 our family moved away from Wales to the Midlands. I had been studying Welsh at school but now was put into a

French class. The teacher could not or would not devote the extra time helping me to catch up with the rest of the group. Instead she sat me at the back of the room and told me to 'get on with something useful'. It was so boring just sitting there that I decided to write down memories of my friends from Wales and the good times we had. That not only helped pass the time during each French lesson, but also set me on the road to a writing career.

Some years ago I had a writer friend, Doug, who I visited in London whenever I could. On one occasion Doug took me into his study and showed me the dozens of folders of notes he had in his files – each folder contained ideas for stories he wanted to write. 'But I'm 71 now Steve and I'm afraid I won't live long enough to finish them.' Two years later he was hit by a vehicle on a zebra crossing and killed. I still miss him, but I take the following messages from the tragedy:

- Do what you love to do.
- Remember 'ichigo, ichie' – Japanese: 'each moment, only once'.

WHAT'S WORTH KNOWING?

The title of this section is also a chapter heading in *Teaching as a Subversive Activity* by Neil Postman and Charles Weingartner. First published in 1969 – shortly before Matthew Lipman began his Philosophy for Children movement – it was hugely critical of the content-laden 'delivery' model of the curriculum that existed in America and the UK at the time, partly because such a curriculum did little to encourage young people to think for themselves. Other commentators, including Sir Ken Robinson (see his talks on YouTube), argue that the British educational system even now could do much more to develop both creative and critical thinking in children across the subject range.

At the start of their chapter Postman and Weingartner posit as a thought experiment the disappearance of all syllabi, curricula and textbooks from every school in the land. Furthermore, from that point on lessons could only be conducted in the form of questions that must help students to understand concepts that will help them survive in a rapidly changing world. They challenge readers to reflect upon this and note down the questions they think would be most worth exploring – a salutary task that you may decide to try for yourself.

It is certainly true that children are rarely given the opportunity to decide for themselves what they would like to learn, let alone consider which questions they feel are most worth asking. Developing a community of enquiry allows that freedom to some extent and helps children distinguish philosophical questions that may be explored through dialogue from, for instance, questions that may be answered through the methods of science or by researching facts. P4C, given the concepts it tackles, also helps children gain a useful perspective in deciding what matters in terms of bringing practical benefit to the way in which they conduct their lives. Exploring moral dilemmas, pondering the idea of freedom, identity and what is real gives a greater depth of meaning to life and helps evolve a sense of ethics that can more surely shape people's values and beliefs and so guide their future decisions and actions.

Discussing the topic of 'what's worth knowing' with the class serves as a useful precursor to the processes that make up a philosophical enquiry. Here are some of the responses from KS2 children I asked about this in several school-based philosophy clubs:

- What are the most important things in life?
- How could we cure all illnesses?
- Where do words come from?
- How do thoughts happen?
- If God is good, why do bad things happen in the world?
- What do I need to know to live a good life?
- What is the best way to learn?
- What are the most useful things we've learned in school and outside school?
- How can I keep being happy?
- How can I live the best life possible?

CHAPTER 2
Jumpstart language for thinking

The importance of language – or more precisely one's *awareness* of the language being used in a philosophical enquiry – cannot be overemphasised. The educationalists Postman and Weingartner (mentioned in the previous chapter), along with many others interested in the field, maintain that each of us creates our own unique world based on our interpretation of the experiences and ideas we encounter. Our perceptions/interpretations and the language we use to frame these shape our reality. Another aspect of this process has been termed 'perception is projection', which is to say that the sense we make of the world is reflected in our ongoing perceptions of it. In our own minds we tend to confirm our belief-structures based on our interpretations of previous experiences. This may be summed up in the idea that 'we see the world not as it is, but as we are' (attributed to various sources).

A key function of any philosophical enquiry is to clarify the language being used by the participants to try to establish a 'shared clarity of meaning' that will ideally lead closer towards the truth: we will leave tackling what 'truth' might mean until later. In order for me to understand you, I need to get a handle on what you mean by what you say, and vice versa. This may seem an obvious point to make but achieving it is often not so easy in practice. Thus, asking for clarification, restating what someone has said, asking for examples, thinking of exceptions, testing words and concepts in other contexts – all of these are valuable 'moves' in philosophy for taking an enquiry forward.

In sharpening up children's awareness and appreciation of language, you may want to try something a lecturer of mine used to do. Whenever he spoke in front of an audience he placed a large sign nearby which read, 'I am responsible for what I say, but not for what you hear.'

It occurs to me that children are well on the way to becoming philosophers when they are prepared to take responsibility for what they say and challenge what they hear.

CREATING A HEALTHY LANGUAGE ENVIRONMENT

This can be achieved by cultivating a certain attitude in the children with regard to the way in which they engage with language in the classroom. Such engagement will be apparent to you and to the children themselves through various 'specific observable behaviours' that will to a large extent constitute the evidence that change-for-the-better is happening in the context of philosophical enquiry and more generally in their learning.

You should encourage the following:

- *Self-confidence.* Because you are giving the children a range of how-to techniques for exploring language and meaning while valuing their thinking, you should see their self-confidence rising as they express their ideas. Further, more self-confident enquirers are not fearful of or embarrassed by being wrong, recognising that this is an inevitable part of the active learning process. The mutually supportive ethos of a community of enquiry is further enhanced by a strong desire to explore ideas, a sense of playfulness and camaraderie, mutual respect and a certain pride in moving closer towards an agreed conclusion or the 'truth'; or in some cases a willingness to disagree.
- *Curiosity.* Increasingly, children will become active enquirers rather than passive receivers of opinions, facts and second-hand wisdom. You should notice that the children question more and display a greater enthusiasm when tackling problems (in various subject areas) coupled with a greater ability to deal with difficulties, frustrations and setbacks.
- *Relevance.* Children's questioning will become increasingly incisive and focused on what they feel is necessary and important

to the topic in hand. More broadly, they may become more interested in ideas that they feel are relevant to their own lives. Be aware that this can sometimes lead to awkward questions – 'But Miss, why *do* we need to know the transformational rules in grammar for forming the passive voice?' My own ploy in a tight situation like this is to assume a thoughtful expression and reply, 'Well, let's see if we can come up with at least six reasons ....'

- *Tentativeness*. This is not about low self-confidence but rather refers to the tendency to become less impulsive. You may find that children are less inclined to snatch at their first thoughts or make snap judgements in responding to a question or problem, or to passively agree with another's viewpoint. They will tend to become more reflective, show a greater willingness to change their minds or admit they were wrong, want to reserve judgement until 'all the evidence is in' and be less likely to accept facts and opinions at face value. That said, active enquirers (and good learners generally) have a degree of respect for 'the facts' while realising that these are often provisional and may change over time.
- *Open-endedness*. Sometimes a philosophical enquiry (and indeed many problems in life) may not be clearly resolved. The outcome may be a partial solution, more questions, confusion or even a feeling that no progress has been made. Children who can think more independently and with a greater degree of self-confidence realise that an inconclusive outcome need not be the end of the matter and that further exploration may well reveal a way through. This willingness not to close matters off prematurely is linked to a tolerance of ambiguity and patience during the process of discovery so that there is no sense of urgency to 'know the right answer right now'. The willingness to leave things open-ended for the time being is coupled with flexibility of thought, creative and critical thinking, inventiveness and the willingness to experiment.
- *'It depends'* thinking. Good learners generally and young philosophers in particular understand that 'right' answers or 'the truth' are often a matter of context. What may be the case in one area of knowledge or of life is not so in another. In addition, such thinkers recognise that different languages (i.e. scientific, metaphysical, political, etc.) influence perceptions and powerfully

shape subjective realities. Further, effective enquirers understand that asking questions is a sign of active curiosity in trying to understand another's worldview and that, when questioned themselves, the response of 'I don't know' is one side of the coin whose other face says, 'But how might we try and find out?'

DEFINITIONS

You can use this as a warm-up game to get the children thinking. Split the class into small groups and give each group a scrap of paper with a word written on it that they have to define. At this stage they are not allowed to look in dictionaries or textbooks but must try to reach an adequate and agreed definition themselves.

Once a group think the task has been completed, further test them in different ways. For example, one group of Y5 children was asked to define 'dog'. They wrote, 'A furry four-legged canine mammal that barks and is Man's best friend.' While appreciating their thinking, you can also challenge it in various ways:

- Do the words 'canine' and 'dog' mean exactly the same thing?
- Are there any other kinds of animals that bark?
- Are wolves, coyotes and hyenas also 'dogs'?
- How do you know that dogs are Man's best friend? (i.e. where did you get that idea from?) Do you know for sure? How can you find out more?
- Are there any hairless breeds of dogs?

Once groups feel they have refined their definitions, pass the scraps of paper round so that every group has the chance to think about and try to define every word. Once that's done, choose one word, display the definitions and support a whole-class discussion to try to refine the definition further.

Take it further
Ask the groups to define more abstract concepts such as courage, love, goodness and friendship. Challenge the children's thinking by asking them to go beyond simply citing examples of, for instance,

courageous behaviour. As you circulate among the groups, test the definitions towards which they are working. For example, if courage is 'doing what you fear to do', what if soldiers could be given a pill that completely took away their fear: would their actions then be courageous? Or what if intelligent robots could be programmed to feel fear but were incapable of feeling pain; could you call them courageous if they did something they feared to do? Or what if a cat defended her litter of kittens against a very savage dog that was much bigger than she was – if she was very frightened but acting purely on instinct, could you call her actions courageous? (See the sample dialogue on page 75.)

Even very familiar things can be surprisingly difficult to define, such as the colour blue, for instance. The scientific definition, in this case of blue light (light within the visible spectrum with a wavelength of around 475 nanometres), is clear and accurate enough but doesn't touch on the quality or human experience of 'blueness'.

Either as children come up with their own definitions, or need to look in the dictionary after all, ask them to notice the *ways* in which their words were defined. One online definition of blue tells us that it is a colour intermediate between green and violet, as of the sky or sea on a sunny day. The strategies here are to try to define blue by mentioning colours that it is not; and to give examples of things that are blue. What other strategies can the children find? Can these strategies be applied to other concepts, such as 'courage', for example?

(Incidentally, one well-known philosophical viewpoint on this matter, most famously associated with John Locke's *An Essay Concerning Human Understanding* is to make a distinction between so-called primary qualities and secondary qualities. Primary qualities are those properties of an object that are not related by definition to perceivers – size, shape, motion, number and solidity. These are qualities that an object has 'in and of itself'. Secondary qualities are those that are dependent on a perceiver: colour, temperature, smell, taste, sound. Because perceivers experience the world subjectively, the question of whether 'blueness' occurs in the mind or is 'really out there' is the topic of ongoing philosophical discussion.[10])

SYNONYMS

Take one of the words that the children have defined and ask them to some up with some synonyms (looking in a thesaurus as necessary). Are these words referring to exactly the same thing? Again using courage as our example, we have; bravery, pluck, valour, fearlessness, intrepidness, nerve, daring, audacity, boldness; dauntlessness, stout-heartedness, heroism, gallantry; backbone, spine, spirit, mettle, determination, fortitude, resolve.

Ask the children to check dictionary definitions to inform their thinking and have them look critically at the ways in which the terms are defined. One definition of courage is 'the ability to do something that frightens one; bravery', while the same source defines bravery as 'courageous behaviour', which seems to me like two sticks leaning against one another to prop themselves up.

Another way of exploring nuances of meaning is to create different contexts in which the terms can be used. Thus someone could be determined to do well in a test but taking the test may not require courageous behaviour.

WHAT'S IN A NAME?

The Canadian philosopher Herbert Marshall McLuhan highlighted the human tendency to feel that we understand something just because we have named it. He called this the libel-label gambit: we 'libel' or do something an injustice by merely naming it rather than thinking about it further; and as the polymath Gregory Bateson asserted, the name is not the thing. Sometimes libel-labelling is done unwittingly and innocently because of the failure to distinguish between the descriptive and the evaluative or judgemental dimensions of words. In his book *Fallacies and Pitfalls of Language: The Language Trap* the philosopher and linguist

S. Morris Engel points out that during the Cold War Western nations described Soviet states as 'totalitarian', a term that carried with it an element of disapproval, whereas to the Russians it was a neutral descriptive term. In other words, there was an implied or hidden judgement about the political regime in Russia contained in the word itself, irrespective of the actual political structure in Russia or what 'Westerners' thought of it.

I came across an amusing example of libel-label recently when a friend mentioned happily that she'd had 'a spontaneous remission' of her MS symptoms, according to her doctor. When she asked him what the term meant he said with uplifting candour, 'The symptoms have gone away by themselves for reasons we don't understand', so allowing her to realise that the phrase was a description of an unknown process rather than a medical explanation of what had taken place in her body.

The danger of failing to question what words mean to different groups of people or individuals can lead to us being influenced by language 'without our permission'. We have mentioned elsewhere the way in which the 'metaphors of education' (page 56) as they are often used now create a certain impression of what teaching and learning should be about and what the purposes of such an education should be (to help us 'run and fight in the global race'). The emotive influence of such terms is based on a political stance driven by an economic imperative, and while we may or may not agree with that stance, the crux of the matter is whether we become aware of what the words are 'up to' or not and, when we do, decide whether or how they might influence us.

There are many ways of helping children to become more aware of the language they use, and to question the intended meanings of words used by others. Here are some suggestions that you can implement immediately:

- Challenge exaggerated language such as 'I hate pasta', 'I'm always getting into trouble', 'Nobody likes me', 'That's a totally stupid thing to say'. The casual use of overstatement or superlatives means that when we really do feel strongly about

something our options for expressing it are more limited and have less impact: the use of extreme terms has watered down their force.
- Check with the children that they have thought about the words they use and know what they mean. As an example, I often come across young writers who will put 'the night was pitch black' into a story and yet rarely do I meet a child who knows what 'pitch' is – some hazard a guess that it's something to do with sound, which confuses them further!
- Make the children aware of what are called 'thought-terminating clichés' or 'thought stoppers'. These are words or phrases that discourage critical thought. They may be used unwittingly or deliberately and are usually short and generic truisms that seem to offer simple answers to complex questions. Because they are usually so familiar and sound like common sense, they may be accepted uncritically and leave the point or topic unexamined. Some that irritate me (rather than some that I hate) are:

> At the end of the day.
> Whatever will be will be.
> Everything happens for a reason.
> What goes around comes around.
> Everyone is entitled to their own opinion.
> You are either with me or against me.
> The will of the people.
> Science shows that … ('It's been clinically proven' is equally annoying).
> Ah well, that's life.
> There's no smoke without fire.

As you will see from the last example, proverbs provide a rich source of thought-stopping platitudes that are also often exaggerations/overstatements:

> A bad penny always turns up.
> All things come to he who waits.
> A word to the wise is enough.
> Behind every great man there's a great woman.
> Good beginnings make good endings.

He knows most who speaks least.
It never rains but it pours.
In for a penny, in for a pound.
Knowledge is power.
Seeing is believing.

NOMINALISATION

This is the act of turning a verb into a noun – creating a name from a process. Since processes are dynamic and names are static, a 'nominalised' concept gives us less information than the verb/process from which it arose. Nominalising has been compared to taking a single snapshot rather than a video clip. The act of 'freezing' things that are constantly changing has indeed been called the photographic effect of language: this is the libel-label gambit in another guise. Once an idea has been made static it's easier to perceive it as being fixed and unchanging and also to forget that it refers to something more complex than the label would suggest. It's significant that throughout their book, Postman and Weingartner talk about 'languaging' rather than just 'language', so emphasising the various interconnected processes that go on, explicitly and implicitly, as we communicate with each other. They also highlight the fact that different subject areas within the curriculum have their own distinct 'languages'; their interest being not so much in the jargon or technical terms of a subject area, but its purposes (structure related to functions), its underpinning assumptions and its embedded metaphors, among other features. Thus they talk about the language of news reporting, the language of science, the language of religion, etc. We might also add to the list 'the language of philosophical enquiry', an important function of which is to take a nominalised idea like 'freedom' and to explore examples of thoughts, feelings and actions ('verbings') that ground the concept in more meaningful real-life experiences.

A phenomenon related to nominalising, and to continue with the photographic metaphor, is 'blurring', which is a kind of generalisation that gives names to classes of things and thereby tends to blur distinctions between individual members of those classes. Thus, for example, I have come across teachers in schools making statements like 'Year Six are a real handful' or 'Children knew how to behave in *my* day' or 'I blame social media for the increased levels of anxiety among young people'.

Blurring, especially if people feel strongly about an issue, can become a kind of prejudice. As I'm writing this book there is a great deal of acrimony in the news between 'Brexiteers' and 'Remainers' with regard to Britain leaving the EU. While these blurred distinctions may be a useful 'shorthand' when talking about the complex matter in question, they can also serve to terminate further thought: it's easy for me to identify with 'the Brexiteers', for example, and thus be opposed to 'the Remainers', or vice versa. If I happen to meet someone belonging to the 'opposite camp' (notice the militaristic metaphor) then I can easily find myself judging him before finding out any details about his view. And notice how blurring can run quietly in the background of our thinking – 'Britain' and 'the EU' are also blurred categories where the temptation may be to tar everyone with the same brush.

In terms of helping children to become more self-aware and effective thinkers, there are several strategies that we can implement immediately.

The philosopher Alfred North Whitehead said that we think in generalities but we live in detail. Explain this idea to the class and point out generalities when they are used. Combine that with precise questioning (see below) to elicit more detailed information as necessary.

SOMBUNALL

The author Robert Anton Wilson coined the term 'sombunall', a useful linguistic tool meaning 'some but not all.' So when you hear someone say, 'Children knew how to behave in my day' you might think to yourself, 'Sombunall children knew how to behave in my day.' Incidentally, Wilson also famously said that belief is the death of intelligence, which is a salutary idea to keep in mind during a philosophical enquiry.

PRECISE QUESTIONING

This is simply a request for further details. For example, recently while travelling into Leicester by bus I overheard a lady say to her companion, 'Of course you can't trust Leicester people.' While I had no inclination to challenge her on this view – she looked pretty fierce – I did think to myself:

- What exactly do you mean by 'Leicester people'?
- In what ways do you think 'Leicester people' are untrustworthy?
- Do you think it's *always* the case that 'Leicester people' can't be trusted?
- What actual experiences have you had which led you to conclude that 'Leicester people' are untrustworthy?
- What has led you to prefix your view with 'of course'?

PLURALISING

This is where we turn a singular into a plural where the singular idea simplifies the issue or is otherwise unhelpful. So we would encourage children to ask questions rather than think of a question; to devise strategies rather than think of a strategy; to explore viewpoints instead of arguing from a viewpoint; to seek solutions instead of a solution; and to pursue meanings rather than look for a meaning. The act of pluralising instantly destroys the assertion that 'there are two sides to an argument' (let alone two side to *every* argument) and the simplistic question, 'Which side of the fence are you on?'

METAPHORS AGAIN

By way of tying up some of the ideas we have just been looking at I want to touch again on metaphors. We have already seen how common educational metaphors come from the world of competitive sport and, frighteningly, from the military – my own junior school teacher used to tell us that we were doing so many 'exercises' in English and maths to 'drill' us for the 11+: on second thoughts that metaphor may come from dentistry rather than from the armed forces.

You may find it useful to reflect on metaphors that you and/or your colleagues rely on when thinking about children's learning. Another familiar cluster of metaphors has been called the 'postal service model' of education. This is where the curriculum is 'packaged' up into discrete subjects, topics and lessons and is then 'delivered' to the children. Our hope is that they 'get it' and hopefully if they do they will gain our 'stamp' of approval. Or consider how we compare intelligence with light, where some children are 'bright' and others (not that we'd tell them so bluntly) are 'dull'. We talk about a 'brilliant' idea or 'illuminating' a subject, not to mention hoping that children will show a 'spark' of interest in our lessons so that they may eventually be 'enlightened'.

An important lesson to be taken from this is that language itself is representative. As the semanticist Alfred Korzybski maintained, 'the map is not the territory' (cf. Gregory Bateson's epithet on page 43), which has profound implications when combined with the notion that language frames our perception of reality. A key feature of doing philosophy in the classroom is to raise children's awareness of these ideas by cultivating in them a relentless pursuit of what their peers mean by the words they use.

ANALOGIES

These are metaphors which, in philosophical enquiry, are used to explore and clarify an idea by looking at the similarities between the things being compared. The 'postal service' analogy with teaching and learning shows a degree of similarity; the way in which knowledge is 'packaged' is analogous to the way in which items are packaged for posting. The way in which a postman feels he has done his job well by delivering a package is analogous to the way sombunall teachers may feel when they have completed a topic and feel that the children have 'got it'.

The usefulness of analogies in philosophy lies in their strength – how numerous and robust the points of comparison are. The delivery model of education has its limitations however, because children cannot stamp 'Return to Sender' on the syllabus (though they can arrange 'fast-track' delivery through extra coaching).

Sometimes analogies are supported by one point of view but rejected by another. A very famous analogy was devised by William Paley, the Christian apologist (i.e. someone offering a defence of a controversial viewpoint), to press the case for a 'Designer God'. Simply put, Paley argued that if you happened to find a watch lying on the ground it would be reasonable to conclude that someone had designed it, whereas it would be unreasonable to think that the components of the watch had been created and assembled by chance processes in nature. In other words, the 'argument from design' asserts that where there is a watch there must be a watchmaker – or as A.A. Milne would have it in *Toad of Toad Hall*, 'Where there's a doormat there must be a door!'

Paley's analogy is rejected by many scientists however; most notably by the evolutionary biologist Richard Dawkins in several of his books, including *The Blind Watchmaker*. Dawkins maintains that a watchmaker envisions the finished watch and the way in which its components will fit together in advance and that the entire process of construction is carried out by the watchmaker. But evolution operating through natural selection is not a purposeful process; evolution is 'not going anywhere' and does not envision outcomes, according to him, so therefore the analogy with the watchmaker is flawed.

The astronomer Fred Hoyle came up with another analogy to try to refute the idea that evolution was purposeless. He asks us to imagine a junkyard containing all the parts needed to make a Boeing 747 (six million of them). A whirlwind blows through, scattering the components about randomly. What are the chances that a fully assembled 747 aircraft will be left in its wake? In the 1982 radio lecture in which Hoyle presents his analogy, he mentions that a colleague of his said that a yeast cell is no less complex than a 747. So if the aeroplane couldn't have been assembled by chance, how could a yeast cell – let alone creatures that are vastly more complex?

If you want to play 'philosophical ping-pong' with the watchmaker analogy further, here are some other points:

- In his essay, Paley maintains that every 'manifestation of contrivance' seen in a watch exists in the works of nature; indeed, such manifestations of contrivance in nature are greater than those seen in a watch and that they 'exceed all computation'.
- A counter-argument asks us to imagine that after finding the watch we came upon a shoe. Would we assume that the watchmaker had also made the shoe, or that there now exists a watchmaker and a shoemaker? If so, then according to the analogy, in nature you would need a cloudmaker for clouds, a treemaker for trees and so on *ad infinitum*. (Personally I find this to be a very weak argument because you can simply assert that God, being God, is the Ultimate Designer and is responsible for the purposeful creation and design of the entire universe.)
- Another argument against the notion of a designer-God says that since all watchmakers have fathers, then God must have a father while the father in turn had a father and so on in infinite regress. The reasoning here is that every effect must have a cause. This idea is based on the rationales of science which do not accept a 'causeless cause'. That idea goes back to Aristotle who postulated the 'unmoved mover' or 'prime mover' in referring to God. As the name suggests, 'the unmoved mover moves other things, but is not itself moved by any prior action'. You can also argue that the notion of cause and effect operates within the material universe and in space-time, whereas God is greater than the universe and exists both within and beyond it (according to some religious viewpoints). Interestingly, although at the present time there are various theories about how the universe came into being, there is no conclusive proof that any of them are true. Typing 'how did the universe begin?' and 'does science accept a causeless cause?' into your search engine will throw up a plethora of interesting articles on the topic.

- A further argument against the watchmaker analogy is that the materials used to make the watch already existed, but theists (people believing there is a God who made and governs all creation) claim that God made things from nothing – *ex nihilo*. A counter to this is that if God is the prime mover and is greater than the universe, then surely it is in His power to create-from-nothing?
- Some thinkers claim that the watch analogy fails because it assumes that because two things share one quality they must have another quality in common. So ….
- A watch is complex. A watch has a watchmaker. The universe is also complex. Therefore the universe has a 'universe maker'. Put in these terms, the final step in the argument doesn't *necessarily* follow. The argument can be clarified by using a further analogy. Leaves are complex structures made from cellulose. Leaves grow on trees. Paper money is also composed of complex structures made from cellulose. Therefore money grows on trees. (A philosophical ping-pong player can be mischievous here and point out that while paper money doesn't grow on trees it's certainly made purposefully out of them.)

And so the arguments continue. I have come across the point that since people have been debating this issue for centuries, even millennia, involving some of the world's finest minds, shouldn't the question have been settled by now? The general response is that philosophy is the attempt to explore concepts and meanings to move closer towards truth. Imagine a large sheet of paper on which is scribbled all the information you need to reach the truth – or 'The Truth'. The paper is tightly folded. The job of philosophy is to unfold the paper and, depending on the issue, this may happen quickly or very slowly, given the complex nature of the ideas involved. It may of course also be that some questions are inherently unanswerable by the human mind, though that doesn't and shouldn't prevent people from talking about them.

For our purposes, which are pragmatic, engaging in such discussions develops children's thinking skills, sharpens their wits, exercises their imaginations and, not least, they are fascinating and fun to think about.

Before we leave analogies for now, it's worth pointing out that even fictional scenarios can offer rich sources of ideas for philosophical questions and subsequent discussion. Thus, using the Terminator films as an example (not that *any* of your children will have seen them), we can ask whether machines could ever become conscious. And do you need consciousness to experience emotions such as love, or to have a sense of morality? Even though the world of the Terminator is a fiction (and, fingers crossed, it always will be!), the concepts arising from looking at that world also exist in real life. Considering whether Arnie's terminator character can understand or experience emotions is no less reasonable a thought experiment than Albert Einstein wondering what the universe would look like if he could travel at the speed of light.

(If you really want to get into fictional worlds and philosophy, check out the Blackwell Philosophy and Pop Culture Series. See References and Resources for the Terminator title, though there are also many more. And for a thorough discussion around machine consciousness, try Chapter 11 of *The Quantum and the Lotus* by Matthieu Ricard, a Buddhist monk, and Trinh Xuan Thuan, an astronomer.)

TRUTH IS LIKE ... BECAUSE

Help the children to understand analogies further by taking an abstract idea and comparing it with something physical. Thus we might say that:

- Truth is like a mountain peak because you have to work hard to reach it.
- Thought is like a stream because it is endlessly flowing.
- Power is like chocolate because some people want more and more of it.
- Hatred is like fire because it burns you up inside.
- Philosophy is like a bloodhound because it's good at sniffing out the truth.

Ask the children to come up with further ideas of their own.

SNAP JUDGEMENTS

It's easy to make snap judgements and simply react to them without further thought. I learned an important lesson years ago as I was about to visit the bank in my home town. From across the street a loud voice shouted out my name. I turned and was horrified to see a scary-looking punk hurrying towards me. His studded black leather gear was complemented by face piercings and a truly spectacular black and purple mohican hairstyle. I immediately decided that this thug was going to mug me and that the best thing to do was to run away or get into the bank fast and hope people in there might help me. Then I wondered why the mugger didn't wait until I'd come *out* of the bank, since I might have more money on me. Then I wondered how he knew me. Then I noticed that he was smiling and holding out his hand (and there was no knife in it).'Mr Bowkett, don't you recognise me? It's Sean D. You taught me English about ten years ago.'

As soon as I recognised him my perspective instantly changed and as I shook his hand I reflected on how dangerous making snap judgements can be. If they are left unexamined (for instance, because I'd run away) they can harden into a prejudice that can colour a person's whole outlook on life.

To round off my little story, over a coffee Sean told me that he was training to become an electrician and had taken a job in a supermarket to help him save for a deposit on a flat, where he and his girlfriend hoped to live once they were married. Sheepishly I told Sean how I had misjudged him. He grinned, nodding. 'I get a lot of that. Actually I did think twice about coming over the road to you – you look pretty alarming in your jacket and jeans.'

When I run emotional resourcefulness workshops in schools I show the children pictures to demonstrate how insidious generalising, stereotyping and prejudging can be. As you might expect, pictures of kittens and other cute creatures get an 'ahhh' from the class, while images of snakes and spiders usually bring out the opposite reaction. This leads into showing pictures of people whose appearance can often elicit a snap judgement, which I follow up by asking the children to consider why they reacted as they did. Not surprisingly, in many cases the children will not have had any direct experience of the kind of person they are (pre)judging; their opinions were formed by what others have said, what they have read in the papers or seen on the news, etc.

PERSPECTIVES

What we think and how we think it largely determines the way in which we view the world – 'We are what we think' as the saying goes. This in itself justifies doing philosophy with children, given that its aim is to explore assumptions, inferences and generalisations in order to come to a clearer apprehension of the truth. This involves trying to understand other people's viewpoints, which are often readily revealed in the language they use.

For instance, a friend of mine is frightened of spiders. Recently when I called to visit her, she answered the door looking anxious and then, immediately, relieved. 'Thank goodness you're here. There's a spider in my bath and it's *huge*! I need someone to get it out.' Heroically I went upstairs to do battle with the beast, only to find that the spider was no bigger than my thumbnail. More seriously, a neighbour of mine 'hates the Welsh'. Notice the extreme language and the vague generalisation encapsulated by the phrase (and see 'Nominalising' on page 46). Such a reaction, which came about in an ordinary over-the-fence conversation, carries a strong emotional charge; my neighbour expressed his 'hatred' with passion. Such a viewpoint also involves 'perceptual filtering', namely the tendency to notice and remember things which support or confirm our beliefs while ignoring other things that run contrary to our opinion or belief.

Examining such 'obserpinions' as I call them – observations welded to opinions – allows us to test their veracity and, to a greater or lesser extent, uncover their origins. Philosophical enquiries aside, showing children how to do this gives them greater control over their thoughts and feelings, and so helps them to become more emotionally resourceful (See 'Outside world, inside world' in *Jumpstart! Wellbeing* for more details).

Techniques of immediate benefit include the following.

Noticing metaphors

Our language is largely built around metaphors (e.g. 'built' and 'around'). These often go unrecognised (i.e. we barely notice or think about them), and yet they have a strong influence on our feelings and how we view the world. I am particularly concerned by the metaphors that crop up in the language of education: we 'push' children and we 'stretch' them, while a teacher I met on a school visit was keen to 'pull' work out of his pupils. We group children into 'cohorts' (an ancient Roman military unit) and offer 'catch-up' programmes to ensure they are not 'left behind' so that we may 'drive up' standards. All of this is because, as a previous education secretary put it, 'we are running and actually fighting in the global race'. When I (metaphorically) get on my hobby-horse about this I suggest using horticultural metaphors instead so that we may plant seeds in children's fertile imaginations; nourish and cultivate them so that they grow and flourish until their efforts bear fruit. Perhaps those who currently use militaristic/sports-based metaphors with regard to children's learning would be willing to turn over a new leaf.

Flagging up exaggerations and extreme language

One way of helping children to assess exaggerations is to show them some synonyms to see if they more accurately describe a viewpoint. While it may be true that my neighbour really does 'hate' the Welsh, it's more likely that the opinion or belief it reflects is not that extreme. Loathe, detest, dislike greatly, abhor, abominate, despise, execrate, feel aversion towards, feel revulsion towards, feel hostile towards, be repelled by, be revolted by, regard with disgust, not be able to bear/stand, be unable to stomach, find intolerable, shudder at, recoil from, shrink from, angered by, annoyed by, irritated by, etc. offers a richer field of thought and the opportunity to more accurately match the emotion to the description.

Exploring the viewpoint through questioning and thought experiments

Again this is not intended to be confrontational, though some people may easily feel threatened by it. I wouldn't, for instance, use the technique with my Welsh-hating neighbour, who seems bigoted and resentful over other matters too – an angry man lives in an angry world.

But taking his viewpoint as an example, we might explore it by asking the following questions:

- What exactly has happened to you to make you feel like this?
- If a baby was born in Wales but to English parents, although the child is Welsh by birth, would you hate him or her as much as if the child was born to Welsh parents?
- Would you hate a person who was born in England but to Welsh parents? What if the family moved to Wales when that person was very young?
- What if you discovered that a long-time friend of yours was Welsh: would that change your feelings towards that person?
- What if a person was born exactly on the Wales/England border: would you hate that person half as much as you hate someone born in Wales?
- What if the son of Welsh parents learned in adulthood that he was adopted and that his biological parents were English: would you feel differently towards that person after his discovery?
- What if a child is born to Welsh parents on an aeroplane flying over international waters? (Some commentators argue that you, or your parents on your behalf, can take the nationality of the country where the plane is registered, or their nationality. Also, apparently, some nations grant citizenship to 'fly-by babies').

CHINESE WHISPERS

This game is played all around the world. A sentence or short anecdote is passed from one person to another with the result that, through mishearing, exaggeration and elaboration the story changes as it circulates, often causing amusement when the final version is compared with the original. As a teaching tool, playing Chinese whispers helps children to understand how apparently minor misconceptions can accumulate and eventually make a big difference so that they can more fully appreciate the impact of gossip and rumour. Apart from that, the activity highlights the importance of careful listening and, in the context of a philosophical enquiry, checking what fellow enquirers mean by what they say.

Tell the children that they must whisper the sentence only once to the next child in line, who is not allowed to ask for it to be repeated. Sentences that have proved popular in the game include:

- I took my dog for a walk today and then I gave him some food.
- The sun has got its hat on and is coming out to play.
- The moon shines on a windswept beach near the foggy sea.
- Dogs dig holes for big bones.
- A bunch of yellow bananas launched on a blue boat.
- Two tiny toads ate fat flying flies.

IN YOUR OWN WORDS

A useful skill in a philosophical enquiry is the ability to restate what someone has said in order to ensure that the meaning has been understood correctly. Note that paraphrasing and summarising are not the same thing. Paraphrasing means to restate someone's ideas in your own words, whereas summarising means to distil only the essential points of what somebody has written or said.

Show the children suitable non-fiction extracts and encourage the use of a dictionary and thesaurus. Ask that they read each extract through a few times and then to set it aside as they write their own version. If a child uses the author's exact words at any point, these should be underlined – point out that this should happen as little as possible. Revisit the activity from time to time, using progressively more difficult extracts. Here are some short examples to start you off, suitable for upper KS2.

1. He gorged on chocolate until he felt nauseous.
2. The price of admission is included in the ticket.
3. The landscape gardens were lush with greenery from May to August.

4. The rambling house had been completely renovated with extensive redecoration.
5. A thunderstorm raged overhead. Flickers of lightning threaded the sky.
6. The family planned a radical declutter before downsizing to a more manageable abode.
7. The upmarket restaurant offered a wide range of international cuisine.
8. Sarcasm is the lowest form of wit: wit is the highest form of humour.
9. His raging temper did little to strengthen the force of his argument.
10. Creative marketing is the key to successful entrepreneurship.

Tip: To cater for differing ages and abilities, select examples from class readers or individual titles that particular children are reading.

SUBTLE DIFFERENCES

A necessary skill for young enquirers is the ability to notice and question nuances of meaning in the language that people use. You can begin to sharpen the children's wits in this way by giving them spot-the-difference challenges using both pictures and words. A huge variety of images is available online, but here's one to start you off (see Figure 2.1).

Continue by asking the children to notice how pairs or groups of words, phrases and sentences differ *in the way they look*. Note that at this stage there's no need for children to understand or explain the differences grammatically or in terms of their meanings. (This takes me back to my own school-days when 'exercises' like these were standard fare.)

here/hear, there/they're, lightning/lightening, past/passed, principle/principal, all together/altogether, awhile/a while, practice/practise, council/counsel, advice/advise.

Figure 2.1
Source: Tony Hitchman

Take it further by showing words that can have a variety of meanings depending on the context. Ask the children to come up with sentences that highlight the differences of meaning. For example, 'plot':

- The gardener dug over his plot of land.
- The criminals thought of a foolproof plot to rob the bank.
- The story had an exciting plot.

Other words include bank, bear, case, club, date, fair, flat, good, interest, light, race, right, sound, spell, tense, well.

Now let us move on to more testing examples of differences in meaning. We looked at synonyms on page 43, and you may want to refer back to that chapter as a precursor to this activity.

Is bravery the same as courage? Is courage the same as fearlessness?

Tip: Offer sample sentences as necessary. For example:

- He showed great bravery in battle.
- She was very brave during her dental check-up.
- He was a courageous fighter.
- She had the courage of her convictions.

Is love the same as 'really like', as in 'I love fish fingers/I really like fish fingers'?

- Is truth the same as honesty?
- Is freedom the same as being able to do whatever you like?
- Is fairness the same as justice?
- Is mind the same as thoughts?
- Is goodness the same as kindness?

Vary the activity by taking a word like 'right' and asking the children for sentences that use it in different ways:

- We all have a right to express an opinion.
- Turn right at the next corner.

- It's right to treat people as you would want them to treat you.
- Right, let's get on with the lesson!

WHAT'S THE POINT?

While I think it is right that correct punctuation and careful syntax can aid enormously in clarifying meaning, I don't subscribe to a 'zero tolerance' approach to errors as children are learning to master its intricacies. Part of that learning is for children to realise that even marginally misplaced punctuation marks can completely change the meaning of a sentence or phrase (see Truss 2003).

Here are some examples. As with the 'Subtle differences' activity, begin by asking the children to notice the differences even if at that point (as it were) they aren't able to explain them.

1. We are going to get her./We are going together.
2. A flying doctor who saved my life …/A flying Doctor Who saved my life.
3. I agreed carefully to analyse the report./I agreed to carefully analyse the report.
4. We went over the crime scene with a fine-tooth comb./We went over the crime scene with a fine toothcomb.
5. Run – man-eating wolves!/Run – man eating wolves!
6. Thanks – your donation just helped someone get a job./Thanks – your donation just helped someone. Get a job.
7. Steve enjoys reading, cooking, cats and listening to music./Steve enjoys reading, cooking cats and listening to music.
8. Let's eat, John./Let's eat John.
9. Earlier I saw a kid napping./Earlier I saw a kidnapping.
10. I'm giving up sweets every day this month./I'm giving up. Sweets every day this month!
11. Phil thought Sophy would do well./Phil, thought Sophy, would do well.

Take it further
The positioning of particular words in a sentence and where the emphasis falls can dramatically change the meaning. Show these

examples to the class and ask the children to restate them in their own words:

a) *Only* I won the game on Monday. (I won the game by myself/by my own efforts.)
b) I *only* won the game on Monday. (Winning the game was all I did on Monday.)
c) I won the game *only* on Monday. (I didn't win the game on any other day.)
d) I won the game on Monday *only*. (It's not a game I play/win every day.)

RHETORIC

Rhetoric is the art of persuasive speaking or writing, making use of a range of figures of speech to give the words extra emotional impact. The term has also taken on the connotation of language that is insincere or that lacks meaningful content, as in 'All we get from politicians is empty rhetoric'.

While it isn't necessary to bombard young philosophers with the vast range of rhetorical devices that exist (and the long names they often have – accismus, enthymeme and paronomasia, to name but a few), children may find it useful to know some of the tricks of the trade so that they aren't influenced unwittingly during discussions.

- *Rhetorical question*. This is a question that is asked for effect rather than in anticipation of an answer. For example, 'You don't expect me to agree, do you?' Sometimes the word 'surely' is added for extra impact – 'Surely you don't expect me to agree, do you?'
- *Exaggeration (hyperbole)*. 'The sweat poured off him', 'I was so cross I nearly exploded', 'That decision was a no-brainer'. The overuse of superlatives contributes to the effect – 'That was the most brilliant meal I've ever eaten', 'Your hat is absolutely stunning!', 'I've burnt the toast, what a disaster!'
- *Stereotyping*. This often takes the form of a generalisation that tries to bolster a point of view: 'Social media are stunting children's social skills.'

- *Repetition of a word or phrase, often in clusters of three for added effect*: 'Education lifted people out of poverty in the past. Education is lifting people out of poverty now. And education will lift people out of poverty in the future.'
- *Use of the impersonal form*. This has the effect of shifting the emphasis (of blame or whatever) from individuals or particular groups: 'Mistakes were made, lessons were learned, new systems have now been put in place.'
- *Epithet*. This is the use of an adjective/adjectival phrase that may also be an exaggeration to complement a noun: 'That was a stunning speech.'
- *Understatement (litotes)*. This often uses the opposite of a word or phrase that is the speaker's true intention: 'I don't completely disagree with your point of view.'
- *Verbiage or wordiness*. The use of long-winded explanations often combined with overblown vocabulary and technical terms. This device can be used to try and confuse or to make the speaker look like an authority on the subject. 'It is imperative you comprehend that the excessive application of jargonistic terminology frequently obfuscates matters leading to excessive incomprehension between parties when engaged in a discussion. So remember, short and simple is best.'

PHIL AND SOPHY

Stories and poems are powerful vehicles for helping children understand abstract concepts and for prompting them to ask searching questions. Some years ago I invented Phil and Sophy as characters that embody traits and attributes useful in philosophical enquiries. Here's a short story suitable for lower KS2.

What's in a name?
Phil, Sophy and her cat Pinkerton had gone to visit Story Owl, one of their closest friends. Story Owl was always fun: if you asked him a question he would often reply with a story. Sometimes you had no idea how the story answered the question – but Story Owl did that on purpose because he wanted you to think it through for yourself.

On this particular visit Story Owl had prepared the most wonderful tea, which everyone enjoyed. It was a proper cooked meal with lots of fresh vegetables and some juicy steamed fish. Afterwards he brought out the fruit bowl. He chose some strawberries, Phil ate a few blueberries and Sophy enjoyed a good helping of gooseberries.

'Ahhh!' said Phil when they had all eaten their fill. He settled down in a big armchair near the fire and folded his hands over his stomach.

Story Owl plumped down in an easy chair very close by.

'And if I could add something to that, my friend – Aaahhhhh!'

Pinkerton curled up between them all and watched the flames in the fireplace. They reminded him of banners and flags and streamers and rags.

'And I'd like to say something too,' he said sleepily after a while.

'What?' Sophy wondered.

And Pinkerton let out a long and contented purrrrrrrrrr.

Then the four friends slept and perhaps they dreamed. Afterwards Pinkerton awoke with a question in his head.

'Phil?'

'Hmm?' He was still half asleep and only just half awake. His voice was all snoodles and snores, mumbles and grumps. 'What, Pinkerton?'

'Well, I can understand why blueberries are called blueberries because I can see that they are blue.'

'That's right I guess.'

'But are strawberries called strawberries because they grow in the straw?'

'Well, that's an interesting question,' said Phil. And he meant it too, but didn't really have the energy to think about it just then.

'And are gooseberries called gooseberries because geese like to eat them?'

'Perhaps ...'

Sophy and Story Owl had also woken up by now and were listening with interest.

'So if that's true, why aren't they called 'geeseberries'? We should call one gooseberry and two or more geeseberries.'

'Pinkerton,' said Phil wearily, 'go back to sleep please.'

But they were all wide awake now and Pinkerton had no intention of stopping.

'And look,' he went on. 'You're resting in an armchair. Is that because it's got arms?'

'I suppose so.'

'Well it's got little legs too, so why isn't it called a "leg chair"?'

'Do you know what I think?' Story Owl looked at Pinkerton with a warm golden gaze, pleased with the little cat's enthusiasm.

'What do you think, Story Owl?' Pinkerton wanted to know.

'I think we should all go for a walk.'

*

Phil, Sophy and Pinkerton scrambled down the trunk of the big oak tree where Story Owl lived. Story Owl himself leapt out of his front door and fluttered to the ground, his feathers making a lovely fluttering sound like the pages of a book flapping quickly in the wind.

'It's funny when you think about it,' said Pinkerton, as the friends walked along the path. He gave a little laugh at all the ideas whirling in his head. 'But things have the strangest names ….'

'Such as?' Sophy wondered.

'Yes, yes! I mean, I am called Pinkerton – but I don't know why.'

'Maybe because of the pink pads on your paws,' Story Owl suggested.

'Or perhaps because you've got a "pinker tongue" than I have,' was Sophy's idea. 'My name is very old and it means a wise person.'

'Well that's true enough Sophy,' Story Owl said with a smile. 'I suppose, when you think about it, what things are called is a very important idea.'

Pinkerton stopped skipping along and shrugged his shoulders. 'Well it's interesting, but is it really important?'

'You silly, ugly little cat!' Phil said suddenly. Pinkerton looked shocked and upset.

'There,' Phil added a moment later, 'I called you a couple of things then that were not very nice. And what I called you and why you thought I did was important to you, wasn't it?'

'Oh, all right,' said Pinkerton, sulking. 'You win.'

'I'm not trying to win. I'm trying to *understand* things.'

'You're right.' Pinkerton was about to say something else when a butterfly flew just above his head. He leaped up and swished at it with his paw.

'Look, a butterfly, a butterfly. Watch it as it flutters by!'

'Maybe it's a kind of fly that likes butter,' Story Owl said. He was enjoying this game of names. 'I agree with you, Phil, that names are very important. Would a rose smell as sweet if we called it a "stenchweed"?'

'Maybe not,' said Phil. 'Well, we've played with Pinkerton's name and Sophy's told you about her name …. But what about you, Story Owl? "Story" is your special name, but what does it mean?'

'It means things that have happened, like "history". And it also means a question – a great quest or journey to find out.'

'But why?' asked Pinkerton.

And Story Owl and Phil and Sophy laughed with love for the little cat.

'Perhaps we can find out tomorrow,' Phil chuckled. 'For now, all of this walking has made me tired again. Let's go back to Story Owl's house so that I can have another sleep in my leg chair!'

*

Phil and Sophy may also be used to illustrate how a dialogue works: how the tension created by opposing viewpoints leads to a deeper exploration of the topic in question.

Phil and Sophy were walking through town. As they crossed the bridge that took them to the park they saw a lady throwing bread to some pigeons. At least 20 of the birds were pecking around her feet. Suddenly a little boy broke away from his mother and began chasing the pigeons, scattering them away in a panic. 'Tony!'

shouted the boy's mother. Straight away he looked guilty and sheepishly went back to her side.

Phil: Did you see that? I guess we've all done things that we know are wrong. That little boy knew he'd done something wrong – did you see the look on his face?

Sophy: Yes. But I wonder. Maybe he just wanted to have fun and play with the pigeons, not knowing that was wrong at all. Perhaps the tone of his mother's voice made him realise that *she* thought it was wrong. But then, it wasn't *very* wrong. Killing someone on purpose would be much more wrong.

Phil: I agree, but I'm still left wondering if we are born knowing what's right and wrong or if we learn it from other people as we grow up.

Sophy: Before we go on I think we need to be clear about the words 'right' and 'wrong'. We are talking about a sense of morality; knowing what we should and shouldn't do. So both of us, for example, know that it's right to be honest and wrong to be dishonest.

Phil: Yes *we* do. But that brings me back to the point about whether we are born with a sense of morality.

Sophy: Babies can't talk yet, so we couldn't ask them! But you say it's wrong to be dishonest. Do you mean it's *always* wrong to be dishonest?

Phil: Well yes, I think I do.

Sophy: And would you say that a lie is a kind of dishonesty?

Phil: Yes.

Sophy: So what if I told a lie say out of kindness? What if I told my friend that I liked her new sweater, even if I didn't, but knowing it would please her and make her feel more confident wearing it?

Phil: A lie is a lie.

Sophy: Yes but would my lie be 'wrong'?

Phil: It would be morally wrong to lie to your friend, even if your motives were good.

Sophy: But if I told her the truth, say, that I hated the sweater, wouldn't it be wrong to deliberately hurt her feelings and maybe even risk our friendship?

Phil: You're caught in a bit of a dilemma there ….

Sophy: And it's easy to say 'a lie is a lie' but life is more complicated than that; in the example I've just given, for instance. We might know as a matter of fact that lying is 'wrong', but in our hearts sometimes we feel that telling a lie is kinder than telling a cruel truth.

Phil: OK, let me sum up so far to be clear. We've wondered if we're born with a moral sense or if we learn it. We've seen how lying is morally wrong even if our motives for lying are good and kind. And I think we both agree that there are different 'degrees' of lying.

Sophy: And that people and relationships are complicated, so to say 'a lie is a lie' is a bit too simple.

Phil: Are you saying I'm simple!

Sophy: No, I'm saying that the *point* you made is too simple. We can know that something is wrong, technically speaking, but still go ahead and do it out of good motives.

Phil: What do you mean by 'technically speaking'?

Sophy: Using the term 'wrong' in the moral sense.

Phil: OK, I understand. But here's a thing. I was watching an action movie the other day and this guy – the hero in the film – killed a bunch of robbers who were going to start shooting people in a bank unless the manager handed over the money.

Sophy: Are you old enough to be watching a film like that?

Phil: Legally, no. But watching the film really got me thinking about this whole question of morality that we're talking about now. So, watching the film was a good thing to do.

Sophy: Well, I'm not so sure.

Phil: But do you think the hero did the right thing – killing evil people to save good people, if that was the only way out of the situation?

Sophy: I think what we're coming to realise is that there are moral *principles*, but that in the real world these can't always be followed, or that there might be exceptions to those principles.

Phil: And by 'principle' you mean?

Sophy: A general guideline, in this case of behaviour, that you intend to follow, although sometimes cannot for all kinds of reasons.

Phil: So that leads me to wonder whether *anyone* could live absolutely according to such principles. I think no one can and that situations will crop up where doing the 'wrong' thing is the 'right' thing to do.

Sophy: I suppose so. But what if morality comes from God – whichever God you happen to believe in? Wouldn't breaking God's Commandments always be wrong?

Phil: Well, whether God exists or not is another big question. Look, here we are at the park. Do you fancy an ice-cream?

Take it further

Split the class into two groups. Have one group put forward Phil's point of view on a given topic and the other group put forward Sophy's. This encourages some children to argue from a perspective that they may not personally share. The value of this is that it offers deeper insight into other views and can lead to the formulation of more incisive counter-arguments.

CHAPTER 3
Jumpstart critical thinking

4 Cs THINKING

While the focus of this chapter is on critical thinking, the ethos of philosophy in the classroom recognises that this must be balanced by other elements in the form of the so-called '4 Cs thinking' model:

- *Caring thinking*, which encourages taking an interest in and respect for the views of others.
- *Collaborative thinking*, which seeks to build on what others have said in order both to open out and deepen an enquiry.
- *Creative thinking*, which incorporates imagination into an enquiry in the form of thought experiments, what-ifs, the use of metaphors and analogies, etc.
- Children will already have done plenty of *critical thinking* through the activities focusing on language earlier. Similarly, as they are introduced to the activities that follow, they will be asked to look closely at the meanings and influences of words and sentences, and hopefully ask many questions about these.

Critical thinking here is used in the sense of 'the ability to make judgements (based on reasoning)', which derives from the Greek word kritikos and krinein, 'to separate, decide'. Critical thinking and creative thinking are sometimes considered as different sets of abilities, though practically speaking they support and complement one another during philosophical enquiries: it takes as much a creative act of imagination to appreciate someone else's viewpoint as it does to challenge it through reasoning.

LOOK CAREFULLY AND THINK

You can use this as a brief warm-up session for the more sophisticated activities that follow. Present these statements one at a time to the class and ask children to jot down any responses and questions that come to mind. The children should work individually on this activity without speaking to their classmates.

1. There's water on the pavement so it must have been raining. (The children could ask about the distribution of water, offer other possible explanations and challenge 'must'.)
2. I believe in UFOs. (UFO stands for 'Unidentified Flying Object', so any aerial phenomenon that you cannot identify qualifies. Many people assume that UFO and flying saucer are synonymous.)
3. The truth as I see it .... (Children may wonder whether this statement is a 'thought stopper' (see page 45) amounting to no more than an unjustified opinion. Asking 'why' may reveal the speaker's reasoning, if it exists.)
4. Children make healthy meals. (This sentence may be read as 'Children cook healthy meals' or 'Children are ingredients in healthy meals'. Well done to the children who can look at the sentence both ways.)
5. The bigger the fire, the more firemen there are. Therefore more firemen cause bigger fires. (The error here is to confuse causation and correlation. Increased numbers of firemen are correlated with bigger fires but do not cause them. Children who have some grasp of this distinction deserve plenty of credit.)
6. This sentence is false. (This is the famous Liar's Paradox. If the sentence is true, then the sentence must be false because it is claiming to be false. However, if the sentence in question is false, then it must be true because the proposition is claiming that it is false.[11] If any child can think around the paradox, he or she has earned a gold star. Any child admitting to a state of confusion also deserves plenty of credit.
7. All's well that ends well. (If you have introduced the notion of 'sombunall' (page 47) to the class, children can use this mental tool to challenge the assertion.)

8. There are two sides to every argument. (Children can question 'every', offer examples of arguments that have more than two sides, or qualify the statement by saying, 'There are *at least* two sides to every argument'.)
9. The grass is green. (Children can point out that grass comes in many shades of green and indeed other colours too. Another ploy would be to ask, 'What do you mean by green?' Very sharp-witted children might say, 'The grass looks green to me, but how do you see it?'
10. Put the box on the table by the window in the kitchen. (This is an example of an ambiguous statement. It could mean, 'Put the box on the table that is by the window in the kitchen', 'Take the box that is on the table and put it by the window in the kitchen or 'Take the box off the table that is by the window and put it in the kitchen'. To try to make these clearer, imagine that there are two tables in the kitchen: one by the window and one elsewhere.)

GIVE ME AN EXAMPLE OF ...

This activity gets the children thinking and helps prime them for the tactics you want them to learn for enquiry sessions.

Give me an example of:

- Something that's always true.
- Something that has just one answer that nobody can argue with.
- Something that was once true but is now no longer true.
- Something that will become true one day.
- Something that may become true one day.
- Something that can never become true.
- Something that's true for some people but not for others.
- Something that is always an opinion.

Tip: These statements are rather vague and, you might decide, even ambiguous. Ideally, children will immediately ask you what you mean by 'true', which could lead to a discussion around that before the activity starts. The examples the children subsequently offer could also spark further questions and debate.

WORKING WITH CONCEPTS

We have already seen that the 'big ideas' forming the basis of much philosophical discussion are vague, abstract notions that require a context for them to have any practical meaning. S. Morris Engel in his *Fallacies and Pitfalls of Language* reminds us that someone with a logical mind would be astonished to hear people talking of 'redness', 'roundness', 'beauty', 'truth', etc. without attaching these qualities to concrete objects. To demonstrate this you might read out a list of such abstractions, slowly and one at a time, then ask the children what they *imagined* in order to process each word. Thus, on hearing the word 'beauty', for example, Phil might imagine a beautiful beach, Sophy might picture her pet cat Pinkerton, whom she loves and thinks is beautiful, Ben might imagine a poem that always moves him and so on.

An important element in any enquiry therefore is to link concepts with contexts. When we want to explore the notion of 'freedom', for instance, we must ask what it means to be free and we do this by offering examples that flesh out the idea and how its meaning changes or deepens depending on the context. This soon develops into the kind of dialogue that lies at the heart of a philosophical enquiry.

Phil: A lion is free because it can roam wherever it likes across the savannah.
Sophy: But it is still at the mercy of its instincts. When it is hungry it *must* hunt.
Phil: That's right. But it is still free to choose which antelope or whatever it wants to try to catch.
Sophy: Well, I wonder. If I remember correctly, lions will try and pick off the weaker animals; those that are very young, or old, or injured. Would any lion choose to attack the alpha male of the herd? That would carry a greater risk of the lion itself being hurt or killed.

Phil: But if a herd of antelope has, say, five old animals and three injured ones and a young one that's wandered away from the group, the lion – though its instinct says it must hunt – can decide which vulnerable animal to attack.

Sophy: What do you mean by 'decide'? Do you mean that the lion thinks to itself, 'Hm, that old antelope is limping. It's also the one that's furthest away from the alpha male. So I'll go for that one'?

Phil: I don't suppose lions think in words like we do, but *something* must happen in its brain to cause it to attack a particular antelope and not any others.

Sophy: Maybe it's instinct again, although it would be difficult to prove I guess.

Phil: I suppose so. We've been thinking about freedom as 'freedom to act', and perhaps it's true that lions and other animals don't have that much freedom to act. But humans have more freedom to act, surely? If I'm hungry – like, *really* hungry, I can still decide to hang on for a bit longer until I finish watching my movie or playing my videogame …

Sophy: Or starting your homework.

Phil: Yeah right, but I don't have the freedom not to do it at all!

My characters Phil and Sophy belong to a philosophy club at school and quickly generate a rich cluster of ideas and further questions around the topic. It's likely that many of the children in your own class will also be able to get their teeth into a topic just as confidently and incisively once they've practised some of the skills. You'll appreciate that the idea of freedom in the context of free will is much deeper than Phil and Sophy have yet touched upon – type 'do animals have free will' into your search engine to pull up all kinds of interesting articles on the subject. You will also quickly pick up other avenues of thought to suggest to the children if they are discussing the matter – but by guiding and gently prompting as a facilitator rather than doing the 'thinking work' for them. (See page 145.)

I'm sure you also realise that the idea of 'freedom' is larger and more multifaceted than the notion of 'freedom to act' or even 'free will'. One way of highlighting this for the class is to ask for sentences where the word 'free' is used:

- I got a free gift in my magazine.
- The big sale at the shop ended up as a free-for-all.
- It's a free country.
- Are you free to go to the cinema tonight?
- The dog's lead became tangled around a branch, but Sophy pulled it free.
- I got the 'get out of jail free' card while playing Monopoly.
- I like to spend my free time reading.

A next step is to try to come to an agreement as to the definition of 'free' in these different contexts. Thus a free gift is one that 'comes without cost' or 'did not cost me extra'. (Sharp-witted children may point out that the phrase 'free gift' is a tautology, since if you are given a gift it cost you nothing, so therefore it is free.) Free in the sense of 'free-for-all' suggests disorganisation and even chaos, so children may wonder – and you can encourage them to – what that has got to do with 'freedom' as a larger idea.

After a discussion you can create a display board of the children's thinking, in this case showing the different kinds or contexts of 'free' or 'freedom' and restrictions placed upon it. One class that had this discussion created a display including free in terms of cost, political freedom (free country), which led on to further discussions of laws and how these related to 'moral' laws such as 'killing is wrong'; freedom of choice versus habits, social rules and conventions ('I am free to dress as I like, but that will never happen because I wouldn't want people to laugh at me.'); free time as opposed to 'free *of* time', and others.

WOULD YOU RATHER ...

This is a familiar warm-up game that encourages children to reflect upon their choices rather than make snap judgements on a whim. Once children are familiar with the idea they can make up their own examples. So would you rather:

1. Meet your favourite cartoon character or a living T. rex?
2. Be able to fly or become invisible at will?

3. Be as good-looking as you wanted or live for 150 years?
4. Win £10,000 or cure your best friend of a serious illness?
5. Own a money tree or find a portal to another world?
6. Have no TV ever or no smartphone ever?
7. Travel into the past or the future (and how far and where to)?
8. Be able to read people's thoughts or make people carry out your commands?
9. Be poor but kind or rich but cruel?
10. Live in a virtual reality world of your choice or this real world?

Take it further
- Leave the choices blank for children to fill in their own. For example: Would you rather meet your favourite xxx or a xxx? Would you rather own a xxx or find a xxx?
- Increase the number of options so that decision making becomes more difficult. Would you rather:
  a) Own a money tree?
  b) Find a portal to another world?
  c) Be granted three wishes by the genie of the lamp?
- Push the ideas further where possible. Thus, for instance, in example 4, increase the amount to £100,000 and imagine that your friend has an incurable illness that will kill him or her within a week.
- Encourage it-depends thinking. Thus, in example 3, the choice might depend on whether your good looks faded with age, and whether you could live healthily for 150 years.
- Explore the broader themes that some of the examples highlight. Thus, example 3 touches on the themes of identity and values. Example 8 raises the issue of power.
- Turn the statements into 'what-ifs' to stimulate further thinking. So, what if there was no technology at all? What if time travel was possible? What if all or certain people could read other people's thoughts?

Tip: If you use the what-if activity as the basis for a discussion, append these three subsidiary questions:

- What would the world be like?
- What problems could there be?

- How might we solve those problems?

Even when what-if scenarios are fantastical (a variety of the thought experiment) they can still touch upon real-world themes and actual problems. For example, during one workshop, the class discussed 'What if people started to shrink when they reached age 30 and that by the time they were 60 they were just a few inches tall?' The children were very quickly talking about what special provision would need to be made for 'little older people' in society, discussing how transport would need to change, how children would need to become much more independent in certain ways and so on. These discussions in turn led to more philosophical reflections around identity, relationships, power and altruism.

A book I would recommend in connection with the would-you-rather and what-if games is Gregory Stock's *The Kids' Book of Questions*. Many of the questions encourage reflectiveness, reasoning and exploration of a number of important philosophical themes. There's a version for adults too.

A MATTER OF OPINION

A key feature of philosophical enquiries, which sets them apart from mere discussion or debate, is the supporting of viewpoints and opinions by evidence and reasoned arguments. These can be highly abstruse: the logic used by professional philosophers can look more like mathematics. For our purposes though it is important for children to understand that doing philosophy is not *just* a matter of opinion or of simple belief. In addition, while the etiquette within a community of enquiry involves respecting what other people have to say, this is not the same as accepting that all opinions are equally 'good'. As the philosopher and educator Will Ord likes to say, be merciful with other enquirers but be merciless in seeking the truth.

It is commonly held that 'everyone is entitled to his own opinion', but this does not imply that all opinions are backed robustly by evidence (facts and examples) and reasoning – a series of logically linked statements leading to a conclusion. Even when an opinion is supported by examples or a 'chain' of reasoning, we may not be convinced if the examples or links in the chain are weak (see 'Strength of reasons' on page 24 and 'Rhetoric' on page 68). For instance, when my neighbour stated that he 'hates the Welsh' (page 55), the reasons he gave were that Welsh fans at a football game he attended laughed when an England player missed a penalty shot, and also that 'the English and the Welsh have been at each others' throats for centuries'. He said these things angrily, but then again the strength of emotions behind a viewpoint is not the same as the strength of reasons used to back it up.

The philosopher Michael LaBossiere offers a refutation that all opinions are equally good in the form of a neat, logical chain: if all opinions are equally good then the opinion that they are not is as good as the opinion that they are. This is a strong sequence of logical links using the 'if-then' pattern of reasoning that offers a useful tool in a philosophical enquiry. Here's an example by a Year 3 group, who within a couple of minutes are probing 'real-life' themes such as wealth, power, freedom, morality and justice:

- If money grew on trees then people who had no gardens would be poor.
- If poor people had no trees then they would steal from the rich.
- If the poor stole from the rich then they'd be put in jail.
- If all the poor were in jail those outside would be equal.
- If all rich people were equal then there would be no need for them to work.
- If the rich did not work then only the poor could work.
- If only the poor worked then they would be the only ones being paid.
- If only the poor were paid they might become richer than the rich.
- If the poor became richer than the rich then we would run out of money.
- If we ran out of money then we would have to plant more trees.

- If we planted more trees then there would be no spare land.
- If there was no spare land then we could not build more houses.
- If we could not build more houses then we would live in the trees.
- If we lived in the trees then we would become like monkeys.
- If we became like monkeys we would groom each other for fleas.

(From *But Why* by S. Stanley with S. Bowkett (2004), used with permission)

Show the class the following chains of reasoning and invite the children to spot any flaws or weaknesses. In addition, if any child feels that an argument is convincing, ask for at least one reason or reasons why.

1. I do not support the borough council introducing car-parking charges because education is important and parents have the right to choose the best schools. The best school for my child is in town. I do some shopping in town once I have dropped my child at school, to buy necessary items like food. Car-parking charges single out parents with school-aged children unfairly. Why should I have to pay to park each day to purchase essentials like food?
2. If it is summer then the days are longer. If the days are longer then children can play outside more. If children can play outside more then they are happier. Therefore, children are happier in the summer.
3. I should be allowed to stay out later in the summer because the days are longer.
4. I should be allowed to stay out later in the summer because I deserve it.
5. If Bertie Bubblebonce wrote the Harry Potter books then he is a great writer. Bertie Bubblebonce did not write the Harry Potter books so therefore he is not a great writer.
6. All oranges are fruits. All fruits grow on trees. Therefore oranges grow on trees.
7. All fruits grow on trees. Tomatoes grow on vines, not on trees. Therefore tomatoes are not fruits.

8. I think, therefore I exist. My shoes exist, therefore they think.
9. All men are mortal. Steve Snugglejumper is a man. Therefore Steve Snugglejumper is mortal.
10. All boys eat apples. Sam eats apples so Sam is a boy.

Some guidance:

1. The writer here chooses to park to shop. She might equally buy groceries online or visit shops where parking is free. Since the proposed car-parking charges apply to everyone, the writer is not being singled out unfairly.
2. The first two statements are matters of fact. The third statement is an assumption that may or not be warranted. It is also an unsupported generalisation: some children may be happier outside, but some may not (see 'Sombunall' on page 47).
3. The reason itself does not fully justify staying out longer. There may be other considerations where coming indoors earlier is preferable.
4. This is an opinion that is not supported by examples or further reasoning.
5. It does not follow that Bertie is not a great writer because he didn't pen the Harry Potter books. He may have written other great books. There would also be some mileage in discussing the meaning of the word 'great'. Does it mean the same as popular and successful?
6. The second statement is an unproven premise. Do all fruits in fact grow on trees? The botanical definition of a fruit would be helpful here.
7. The same consideration applies here. The first premise is false – not all fruits grow on trees. The second premise is sound, but the conclusion is false.
8. The first statement is based on Descartes' famous dictum, 'I think, therefore I am' (Cogito ergo sum). The second statement is sound (unless you want to discuss what it means to exist), but the conclusion is unsound.
9. This is an example of a valid argument where a sound conclusion is the consequence of two sound premises.
10. The first assumption is unsound and leads to an unsound conclusion.

A SAMPLE ARGUMENT: VIOLENCE IN VIDEOGAMES

Below are 36 statements on the topic of the pros and cons of violence in videogames. You might choose to show the class a selection of these and ask the children to express their opinions about them, justifying what they say as far as possible. Also point out examples of rhetoric used to bolster any view (see page 63).

Take it further
You can ask the children to explore the issue more thoroughly by creating a grid of 36 cells and placing a statement in each according to the numbering shown (also refer to Figure 3.1).

Note that the infoscraps around the issue of violence in videogames is suitable for Upper KS2 (and Lower KS3). Fewer infoscraps that are conceptually easier to understand and think about can be created quite easily for younger children.

1.6	2.6	3.6	4.6	5.6	6.6
1.5	2.5	3.5	4.5	5.5	6.5
1.4	2.4	3.4	4.4	5.4	6.4
1.3	2.3	3.3	4.3	5.3	6.3
1.2	2.2	3.2	4.2	5.2	6.2
1.1	2.1	3.1	4.1	5.1	6.1

Figure 3.1

Photocopy some sets of the statements in their boxes and cut these out (or ask the children to volunteer for the job). Split the class into groups and give each group a set of 'infoscraps', which they are encouraged to arrange and rearrange on a tabletop in different ways according to the tasks you set. For example:

- Arrange the infoscraps into two piles headed 'I agree' and 'I disagree'. Children will need to come to a consensus as far as possible to do this.

- Refine the task by using a five-point scale – I strongly agree/I agree/I neither agree nor disagree/I disagree/I strongly disagree. Children may find it harder to reach a consensus here, so each child in a group may be allowed to make her own choice irrespective of others in the group.
- Sort the infoscraps into two piles, Fact and Opinion. Further sort the infoscraps into those whose supporting reasoning is sound and those that are weakly or unsupported by reasons.
- Give each group the opportunity to take away a number of infoscraps and replace them with statements of their own. These might support a group's joint opinion or an opposing viewpoint.
- Select infoscraps which exemplify different tactics for winning an argument, such as an appeal to authority, an appeal to statistics, attacking individuals rather than their viewpoint (*ad hominem*), etc. (see page 63).

You might consider asking the children to create further sets of infoscraps based on enquiries you run with them. These will form a useful resource for other classes. Note that the videogame topic grid is 6x6 cells to allow for the use of dice rolls if you wanted to introduce the random factor into children's analysis of the points. Subsequent grids can feature as many or as few cells as you wish.

INFOSCRAPS

1.1 Violence exists in the real world. Experiencing violence in videogames helps us to understand it better. Therefore playing such games is a good thing.

1.2 People who start playing violent videogames will get bored and want more extreme violence in their games in future.

1.3 Professor Gerry Mander of Camford University, an expert on violence in videogames, says playing videogames is a bad thing.

1.4 In the Bible it says 'an eye for an eye and a tooth for a tooth'. It's much better to adopt that attitude by being angry or violent in a videogame than in real life.

1.5 Human beings are violent creatures and need some way of letting off steam. Playing videogames is a harmless way of doing this.

1.6 My father's best friend Ben Leech has been playing violent videogames for years and he goes to church.

2.1 The time you spend playing videogames is time you could have spent doing something more constructive.

2.2 Violent videogames, where you have to defeat the bad guys, help to teach us more about what it means to be good. Without evil we cannot measure goodness.

2.3 Playing videogames helps me to relax and also 'recharge my batteries' ready to concentrate more at school. Therefore playing videogames is a good thing.

2.4 I know kids of 11 or 12 who play 18-rated videogames, and it doesn't seem to have harmed them.

2.5 There was an item on the news about a 16-year-old boy who robbed a newsagent's shop at knifepoint. Police found violent videogames in his bedroom. Therefore we have proof that such games can cause some people to commit crimes.

2.6 Playing videogames helps you keep your wits and reflexes sharp. That must be a good thing if you want to get better at certain sports.

3.1 Some people are just born violent, so banning videogames will have no effect on them. It may even make them worse because they would feel frustrated if they cannot play.

3.2 Banning certain videogames (or films, books, etc.) is a violation of human rights and therefore wrong.

3.3 The government has a responsibility of care towards the citizens of this country. This includes protecting them from the negative influence of videogames.

3.4 A study some years ago showed that playing violent videogames caused people to make 'impulsive bad choices'. So it was a case of 'shoot first and ask questions later'.

3.5 Every time someone who plays violent videogames does something kind and good in the real world is further evidence that such games are not harmful.

3.6 Most people can tell fantasy from reality. I mean, you wouldn't really go round with a machine-gun killing people, would you?

4.1 Soldiers should be allowed to play shoot-em-up games as this helps prepare them for combat.
4.2 If there is just one proven case of violent videogames leading to violence in real life, then they should be banned.
4.3 If playing videogames helps people to get rid of violent feelings harmlessly, then this would make the world a more peaceful place. Therefore banning such games is wrong.
4.4 Any time that violent people spend playing videogames means they are not out on the streets doing real violence.
4.5 In videogames you can do violent things and not face the consequences. This means you don't think about the effects of your actions. Therefore such games are a bad thing.
4.6 The world is clearly becoming a more violent place. Our country will need more soldiers to defend us. One way of training them is to use simulations of real battle situations. Videogames can achieve this at little cost.
5.1 Because some of today's children will become the soldiers of tomorrow, it makes sense that such children should be allowed to play violent videogames to begin training them early.
5.2 If videogames were just about doing nice, kind things, they'd be boring and nobody would play them.
5.3 Children should be encouraged to play videogames where only good things happen, as this would show people how to be good citizens.
5.4 My dad's cousin was going through depression and said that playing violent videogames helped him to get through it. Therefore such games are a good thing.
5.5 Unless the spread of violent videogames isn't stopped it will get out of control. In the end, violent maniacs will overrun the world.
5.6 Doctor Reggie Tarian of Kenniston University says playing violent videogames is good for you. The man is clearly an idiot. Also, three years ago he was in court on a tax evasion charge. How can the opinion of such a man be trusted?
6.1 In Ancient Rome allowing people to watch gladiators killing each other didn't make Rome a less violent place. It follows that allowing people to play violent videogames will also not lead to today's society becoming less violent.

6.2 Most people when asked say they don't think that violent videogames are bad, so it would be going against the will of the people to ban such games.

6.3 Statistics show that older people don't understand modern technology, so their opinions about videogames are less important. Besides, *they're* OK aren't they with their pensions and savings and mortgages paid off? That really makes my blood boil!

6.4 A violent videogame, once bought, can last for years. That's much cheaper than paying to see violent films on DVD or at the cinema. Therefore videogames are preferable to the cinema and DVDs.

6.5 You're either for violent videogames or against them. Most reasonable people are for them. Surely that must count for something?

6.6. Shakespeare's plays are full of violence and people think he's a genius. How is the violence in *Macbeth* different from the violence in a lot of today's videogames?

Commentary on the statements
Feel free to agree or disagree (or strongly agree/disagree).

1.1 The first premise is sound. The second premise is questionable and so the conclusion is not sound.

1.2 Here is a useful place to use the mental tool 'sombunall' ('some but not all', page 47) and 'perhaps'.

1.3 This is an 'appeal to authority'. We would also want to know in more detail how Professor Mander reached his conclusion.

1.4 This is another appeal to authority, though of a different kind. The Bible is such a diverse and complex set of writings that you may often find a quote to support your viewpoint. Contradictory quotes may also exist; in this case, 'turn the other cheek' (though you would lose the videogame if you did).

1.5 You might argue that some human beings are violent while others are peace loving. While we might accept that some people need to 'let off steam', playing violent videogames may not be the most constructive way of doing this.

1.6 The fact that Ben Leech goes to church and plays violent videogames does not refute reasons for wanting a ban on such games. You may argue that people are complex and that the apparently 'good' act of going to church and the arguably 'bad' act of playing violent videogames can both form part of a person's psyche. It's also possible of course that Ben Leech is insincere in his churchgoing and attends for the sake of appearances.

2.1 The point is true enough as far as it goes. Equally you could argue that time spent playing videogames would keep bad people off the streets where they might do criminal or violent things for real.

2.2 Some precise questioning would help here. In what ways exactly does playing a violent videogame teach us more about being good? Define 'good'. Many such games do not touch on concepts of justice and responsibility – except indirectly where killing opponents can earn you points and other rewards. Is there scope for kindness in any games of this kind that you can name? If I was playing such a game and tried to help an opponent, wouldn't he or she or others simply try to kill me? As such being kind or showing mercy would make me vulnerable: is that the kind of message you want children to pick up?

2.3 While we might accept this point we could question the generalised conclusion.

2.4 We could ask how this assertion supports the broad argument that 'playing violent videogames does not cause harm'. We could equally suggest that there are likely young children playing games designed for adults who have been harmed by them (becoming desensitised to violence or otherwise emotionally damaged); so the two viewpoints cancel each other out.

2.5 This is cherry-picking an example to support a viewpoint. We could ask whether it's possible that young offenders exist in whose bedrooms violent videogames were *not* found. We could also ask whether, in the case of this particular youth, other kinds of violent material were also found (*Macbeth*, for example: see point 6.6), and whether they are responsible for the person's crime – and if so, how can we prove this?

2.6 We could ask for studies that support this assertion. We could also argue that, even if we accepted the point, violent videogames do not teach sportsmanship. Further, many sports demand a degree of physical fitness that playing videogames does not offer; quite the reverse in fact. Many sports also demand teamwork. We may wonder whether being in a 'team' when involved in an online multiplayer game is similar to being in a sports team.

3.1 Here we would simply ask for proof that 'some people are born violent'. If it can be proven that violence is genetic it opens up the whole nature/nurture debate, which in turn leads into the free-will discussion – 'Yes I murdered my wife Your Lordship, but I couldn't help it. My genes meant I couldn't help it. So I'm not responsible.' If free will does not exist, as some scientists and philosophers claim, then the my-genes-made-me-do-it argument needs to be resolved or else the entire justice system will collapse. (Note however that according to Wikipedia the possible genetic basis for altruism in humans is not the same as the philosophical issue of altruism. Type 'the genetic basis for altruism' for plenty of information on this topic.)

3.2 Some time should be spent looking at what the Declaration of Human Rights actually says. One such right says that all people are born equal in dignity and rights. If any case can be shown where playing a violent videogame led to someone violating another person's human rights, then isn't that a strong reason for banning violent videogames, especially since we could argue that the right to freedom, dignity, etc. brings greater good to the world than a right which allows carrying out acts (playing videogames leading to violence in the real world) that cause harm?

3.3 We could ask for evidence that playing violent videogames has 'negative effects' to support the notion that censoring them is part of the government's duty of care. We could further argue that age-rating videogames (and films, etc.) is a reasonable compromise between the government carrying out its duty of care and allowing individuals freedom of choice in society. This point also raises the issue of where the responsibility lies, or how it should be distributed, when it comes to the issue of children's exposure to material with violent content. An extension of the point is to wonder whether, and how, such age-rating of material could ever be enforced.

3.4 We would want more information about the study to assess whether it supports the shoot-now-ask-questions-later argument. Further, does this study or others report any beneficial effects of playing videogames?

3.5 We might argue that this point illustrates that people are complex creatures who are potentially capable of doing both good and bad things. How exactly does the point count as evidence in the broad argument that videogames should or should not be banned?

3.6 We might question the use of 'most' here. How do you know? We could also invoke the whole 'map of reality/perception-is-projection' issue with regard to making a distinction between fantasy and reality – though this might lead to us being accused of drifting from the point.

4.1 We might ask exactly how soldiers are being prepared for combat by playing violent videogames, and whether or how videogames differ from, say, a flight simulator or simulators designed to develop useful skills. We could also invoke points 1.3, 3.4 and 4.5 to try to counter the argument.

4.2 By the same token, if there is just one proven case where reading the Scriptures or Shakespeare led to an act of violence in the real world, then surely this material should also be banned? The point can be deepened by enquiring as to the 'degree of good' a given example brings into the world. We could argue that while Shakespeare's plays do contain sometimes brutal and graphic violence, all in all the Bard's plays bring much more good into the world than videogames, for example, by exploring the very themes of interest to philosophers and by bringing pleasure to millions of people.

4.3 We might question whether releasing (or just expressing?) violent feelings is truly harmless and whether such release or expression means that people will *necessarily* be less violent in the real world. If we invoke the argument that 'an angry man lives in an angry world' then it may be the case that such a man would enjoy the violence when playing a videogame but also carry out violent acts in the real world.

4.4 We could assert that while we accept the point, any time that violent people spend playing videogames could be desensitising them to violent behaviour generally while perhaps teaching them more diverse ways of being violent. We might challenge this point by arguing that many people would not be desensitised to violence by playing videogames because such gameplay has no *consequences* in the real world. If I kill 20 avatars in a game I have not done anything wrong as far as the real world is concerned and so will not face any kind of punishment, but I am still aware of the inherent wrongness of harming a person in real life and sensitive to the fact that the act of harming has consequences.

4.5 We could invoke point 3.6 here. We can also assert that while people don't face the consequences of their actions in such games (i.e. they can kill without facing justice) because the rule of law exists in society, and most people (surely) realise this, they would in many or most cases reflect upon potential courses of action before carrying them out. A counter-argument is that some people, those who are drunk, for instance, don't think about their violent actions beforehand; they just lash out. We might counter this by asking how this supports the argument that videogames are a bad thing. Our opponent might counter *that* point by invoking point 3.4.

4.6 We might accept this point but ask what it has to do with the debate about violent videogames more generally. What may be beneficial in a military context need not be so in the larger society.

5.1 We may ask what particular kind of sense it makes to 'start children early' playing violent videogames. We could also argue that children's innocence is a precious thing and should be preserved as far as possible through childhood.

5.2 We might accept this point in itself, but the discussion is about violent videogames. Besides, the boring nature of 'nice' games does not per se support the banning of violent games.

5.3 We can invoke point 5.2 here. We may also argue that since violence exists in society anyway, children will surely be exposed to bad things. In addition, if many or most children know the difference between fantasy and reality (with the implication that fantasy is 'less real'), then would lessons learned about being a good citizen in a fantasy context be beneficially translated into actual behaviour in society?

5.4 This draws a general conclusion from a single example. We might also question the validity of hearsay/anecdotal evidence and ask if there may have been other and more crucial factors in curing the person of his depression.

5.5 This is an appeal to our emotions through the use of persuader words/emotive language. Such a tactic should always be challenged in a philosophical enquiry.

5.6 This is called an argument 'against the man' (an *ad hominem* argument), where a personal attack is used against someone holding a particular viewpoint. It is a shabby tactic. Further, what connection does Doctor Tarian's tax issues have with the point in question? It is also the case that a person can be reliable and trustworthy in one area of their lives but less so in another.

6.1 The veracity of this analogy can be questioned. How do we know that watching gladiators in the arena did not lead to some instances of Roman citizens becoming less violent? How does it follow that the nature and levels of violence in Ancient Rome have a bearing on violence in modern society?

6.2 This argument uses an 'appeal to the people' (*ad populum*) and exploits the assumption that if the majority of people hold a certain viewpoint they must be right. We might also ask how the person making the point *knows* what 'most people' think in this case. In addition, the phrase 'the will of the people' is a thought stopper (see page 45) unless we spot it and question it.

6.3 The use of statistics in a philosophical discussion should always be questioned. What is the source of the statistics? How exactly do they support your case? We might also ask for other evidence that 'older people' don't understand 'modern technology'. How exactly does this suggested lack of understanding weaken any opinions they may have with regard to the issue of violent videogames? Further, how is a person's degree of understanding of technology related to the moral issues around violent videogames? We would also question how the arguer's rant at the end of this point supports their viewpoint.

6.4 This is an appeal to cost, carrying the assumption that 'less expensive is better'. We may wonder what that has got to do with the ethical implications surrounding violence in videogames. Further, a violent DVD may well cost less than a violent videogame and can be watched many times, so the appeal to cost fails here too.

6.5 This is an example of the 'there-are-two-sides-to-every-argument' tactic and can immediately be challenged – I may agree with some of the points you have made but not others. We may also question how it can be known that 'most people' are for violent videogames and further ask what is meant by 'reasonable' here. Note also the rhetorical tactic of using 'surely' as a persuader word.

6.6 The analogy with Shakespeare's plays is shaky. The nature of violence in the Bard's work and in videogames would be a debate in its own right.

FIVE PRESSURES THAT CAN INHIBIT CHILDREN FROM TAKING PART IN CLASS DISCUSSIONS

As you will see, these 'pressures' overlap. While the causes are not always fully under a teacher's control, the ethos that you establish in the classroom can go a long way towards helping children feel less anxious and inhibited. It's true that some classroom situations, for example, a test, can potentially be more stress-inducing than an ordinary lesson. However, you can point out that a philosophical enquiry is not at all the same as a test and that the aim is for children to feel relaxed and alert as they enjoy taking part in the discussion. (See Jumpstart! Wellbeing for many techniques in helping children to achieve this state.)

1. Right-answer pressure

Sometimes both children and teachers predicate pupils' success on the number of questions they can answer correctly, often by recalling facts that they have previously been told. Children who do not remember may not want to take the perceived risk of 'having a go' and being wrong. By extension, they may be equally reluctant to express an opinion, justify it, give an example, ask a question, etc for the same reasons. It is important therefore to reinforce key elements of the spirit of a philosophical enquiry – that everyone's thinking is valued, that it's fine to change your mind and that any challenge or counter-argument is against the point being made and not the person who made it.

2. Classroom environment pressure

This sometimes shows itself if children don't know 'where the lines are drawn'. On a personal note, when I was a trainee teacher one mentor advised me always to be 'firm but fair'. The teacher and educational journalist Mark Phillips develops this idea by saying that the challenge is in establishing an emotionally safe environment without relinquishing your role as the teacher; by creating the right balance of being emotionally open and authentic without sacrificing the boundaries and role definitions of teacher and pupil.[12] A teacher colleague, whose words stick in my memory, told me that he always aimed to be a 'caring presence' in the classroom, even though he sometimes needed to 'lay down the law' and re-establish the rules and who was boss. He was one of the strictest disciplinarians in the school, but also one of the best-liked members of staff. Sue Cowley's *Getting the Buggers to Behave* is a useful compendium of advice; also check out 'Tom Bennett on the TES Behaviour Forum' online.

3. Peer pressure

This is a complex and potentially very inhibiting, even damaging, influence on some children. A stepping-stone towards easing peer pressure is to explain that we are all different and unique; that one person may be very good in some subject areas and not so good in others, and that applies to all of us. This idea is reinforced by Howard Gardner's notion of 'multiple intelligences' (rather than one fixed general intelligence akin to I.Q.). Gardner's original proposition was that each of us has 'eight ways of knowing'. Thus, for instance, linguistic intelligence is a person's ability to understand spoken and written language and to read and write effectively. Someone who is 'intrapersonally' intelligent is relatively inward looking and good at working out their own feelings, motivations and goals.

It has to be said that the idea of multiple intelligence does have its detractors and that it very much remains a theory that is not yet backed up by a robust body of evidence and experiment.[13] Even so, it is clear that as children grow, their interests develop along with their increasing disinterest in certain things (for whatever reasons). A friend of mine can take a car engine apart and reassemble it, whereas I wouldn't know how to start. That same friend takes little interest in reading and struggles to compose a coherent paragraph, whereas I love the world of language and ideas.

There are scores of techniques for handling the issue of peer pressure (see e.g. Jumpstart! Thinking Skills and Problem Solving, Section 5, for tips on boosting children's emotional resourcefulness). Beyond this, whole-school policy can have a powerful effect on developing 'positive peer pressure', where pupils themselves are encouraged to motivate their classmates to behave appropriately. Again you will find plenty of theoretical background and practical resources online.

4. Curriculum pressure

Pressure on teachers to 'deliver' the curriculum remains high, and on children to try to understand, retain and recall what they are taught. Strategies and resources mentioned above can help children to cope, but the issue is ongoing and not likely to be resolved soon given the political agenda underpinning the educational system. Cogent arguments for wide-ranging changes in the way children are educated have been put forward by, for example, Professor Ken Robinson (you'll find his views presented in a number of talks on YouTube) and in *The Unfinished Revolution* by John Abbott and Terry Ryan.

5. Exam pressure

What applies to the curriculum overall applies here, with the pressure to do well in exams affecting some children very badly. (I once ran a writing workshop with a new Year 6 group as part of the school's book week in October. I asked one boy how he liked being in Year 6 and he said, 'I'm worrying about the SATs.' That, really, sums up the seriousness of the issue.)

It is worth pointing out to your class that the thinking and communication skills they will learn within a community of enquiry will help them understand and respond to exam questions more effectively. They will also be in a better position to realise that assessment of their learning through exams is (for the foreseeable future) an inevitable part of school life, and that revision techniques can be of great benefit in helping children prepare for the test. See, for example, Simon Percival's *The Practical Guide to Revision Techniques*; there are also many others.

Coincidentally, as I was writing this section an item appeared on the BBC News website – Why high-flying Singapore wants more than grades – flagging up the move towards developing resiliency and a positive outlook in pupils. Dr Lim Lai Cheng, Director at the Singapore Management University, advocates the push for character as well as qualifications and the encouragement of well-being in the classroom. Currently, Singapore is in top place in the international rankings for education, but now the powers-that-be recognise that to develop further the educational system must encourage a culture that builds positive emotions, enhances personal resilience, promotes mindfulness and encourages a healthy lifestyle. Perhaps, since successive UK governments have traditionally looked at other countries' educational systems for new initiatives, Britain may soon follow Singapore's lead.[14]

OVERSIMPLIFICATION

We have already looked at the linguistic minefield that can be created by jargon, rhetoric, spin and the deliberate use of obfuscation through the application of overly complex syntactical structures (see what I mean?). A similar problem in striving towards clarity of meaning is the unquestioned use of oversimplification during an enquiry. The solution is to use philosophical 'moves' (tactics) to challenge examples when they crop up – by restating what you think the speaker means, by asking the speaker to define particular words, by offering similar terms so that subtle distinctions can be discussed and so on.

Oversimplification can take a number of forms. We've already looked at generalisations (page 99), but here are some more that you can ask the children to challenge:

1. Children think clowns are scary.
2. Cats and humans are mammals.
3. All birds have wings.
4. Trees put oxygen into the atmosphere.
5. I work in the morning when the light is better.
6. Most young people prefer fruit to vegetables.
7. Shouting always means you've lost the argument.
8. Fish like to swim.
9. Most animals don't live as long as humans do.
10. Half a loaf is better than none.

Commentary on the generalisations/simplifications
1. Challenge this statement by asking whether the speaker means all children, some, a small minority, etc. Also query how the speaker knows this. Is it based on anecdote, research or direct experience? If based on research, ask for the sources.
2. This is a simple statement of fact (rather than an evaluative statement) that can be verified by checking the biological definitions of the terms.
3. Generalisations can serve as a powerful shorthand during communications. This seems like another simple statement of fact, as in statement 2. It would be wise to check if the speaker is suggesting that because all birds have wings (which is true) then all birds can fly (which is not so).
4. This is a fact, though the word 'put' is vague and the questioner may want to know more about the process by which trees (and other plants) release oxygen into the atmosphere.
5. The implication here is that the light is *always* better in the morning, so we might wonder how that could be.
6. As with statement 1, we would want to find out how the speaker knows this. Certain 'clue words' flag up generalisations: sometimes, always, never, most, many, some, all, generally, seldom, none.
7. Spot the clue word. We would also want to reflect on instances when this may not be so, as when a speaker whose microphone has failed needs to raise his voice to a member of the audience sitting in the back row.

8. An immediate problem is the word 'like'. This is a personification that attributes the human quality of 'liking' to fish. We might also query whether the speaker is suggesting that all fish (like to) swim.
9. The word 'most' clues us into the generalised nature of the statement. The enquiring mind may want to know of exceptions that would make the statement more robust and therefore acceptable.
10. Those who enjoy playing with ideas may enjoy thinking of exceptions; for instance, when mould on bread triggers allergic reactions or respiratory conditions. We also recognise that the proverb is a metaphor, so some examples of situations where its wisdom applies would be useful – 'But Miss, I've done *half* of my homework!'

In a philosophical enquiry generalisations (and other kinds of statements) are 'true' if they are supported by facts, backed up by the speaker's own experience, agree with what you know or can investigate about the topic, can be proven with several examples, and are supported by logic and reasoning.

Let me reiterate here though that logical reasoning is not always sound, which is to say that a chain of reasoning may be valid in the technical sense without being true. One of the most familiar 'patterns' of logical reasoning is the syllogism, where a conclusion is drawn based on two initial propositions or premises. A famous example is:

> All men are mortal.
> Socrates was a man.
> Therefore Socrates was mortal.

We can say that the conclusion here is valid because the premises are also valid, as far as we understand them to be (though could Socrates have been a woman writing under a pen name, as did George Eliot?). However, S. Morris Engel (in *Fallacies and Pitfalls of Language*) warns us to be cautious even of syllogisms that appear to be sound. For instance, we can accept that:

All dogs are animals.
All wolves are dogs.
Therefore all wolves are animals.

But if we unthinkingly accept this A+B=C pattern we would be forced to agree that:

All dogs are animals.
All cats are animals.
Therefore all dogs are cats.

The message to the children then is that during a philosophical enquiry, stop – think – question.

ABSTRACTIONS

General terms are also abstractions; more or less vague ideas rather than specific events featuring particular details. We can recognise 'levels' or degrees of abstraction, as in the following example:

Living things – animals – chordates (having backbones) – mammals – carnivores – Felidae (family of cats) – domestic cats – shorthair cats – my cat Mog.

Representing these levels of abstraction visually, we can see that the greatest degree of abstraction equates with the broadest generalisation, or largest category/class, and that moving towards the particular means thinking of ever-smaller categories or classes of things.

Specific, particular

My cat Meg

Shorthair cats

Domestic cats

Felidae

Carnivores

Mammals

Chordates

Animals

Living things

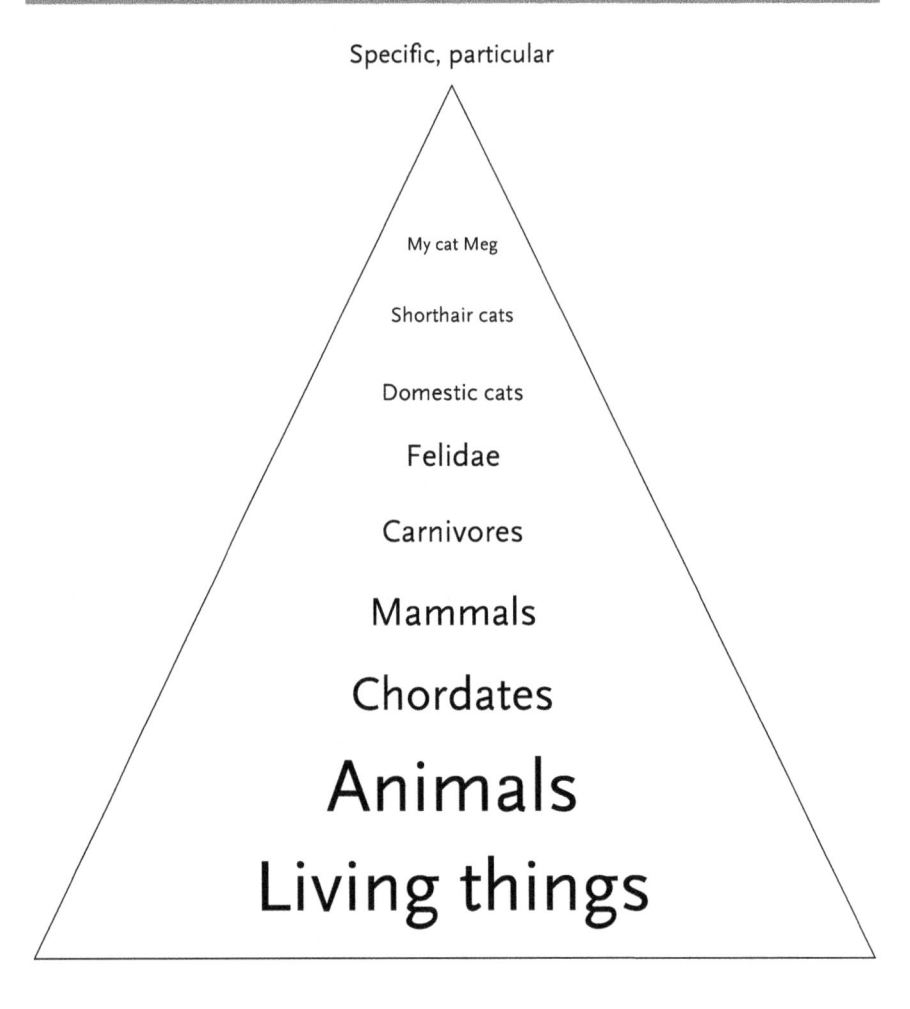

General, vague, high level of abstraction

Figure 3.2

Imagine now that the pyramid is conical and transparent and you're looking down through it from the top. The different levels of abstraction can be represented as circles of increasing diameter, with 'living things' forming the base of the pyramid.

Jumpstart critical thinking

Living things

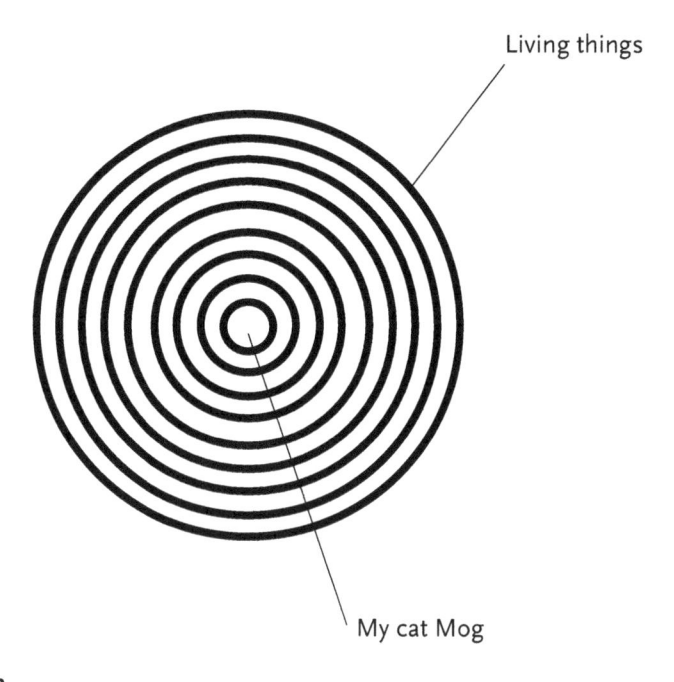

My cat Mog

Figure 3.3

We can use this kind of visual organiser to check the validity of the syllogisms above.

>All men are mortal.
>Socrates was a man.
>Therefore Socrates was mortal.

Clearly 'Socrates' is a sub-class of 'men', which is a sub-class of 'mortal things'; therefore 'Socrates' fits into the class of 'mortal things'. The next example, 'All dogs are animals. All wolves are dogs. Therefore all wolves are animals' fits into the same pattern. However:

>All dogs are animals.
>All cats are animals.
>Therefore all dogs are cats.

We can see at a glance that 'dogs' and 'cats' are separate subclasses of 'animals', and therefore that the reasoning of the syllogism is not sound.

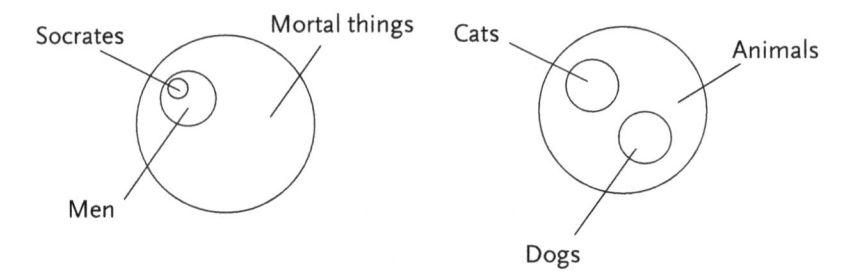

Figure 3.4

Take it further by asking the children to draw their own 'syllogism circles' to see if the following examples are sound.

a) All dogs have four legs. Shep is a dog. Therefore Shep has four legs.

The largest circle is 'four-legged things'. The subclass 'dogs' fits inside this, while the smallest category 'Shep' fits inside 'dogs'. If a child says, 'But what if Shep lost a leg in an accident', give him some credit before asking how that affects the validity of the syllogism.

b) All dogs have four legs. Shep has four legs. Therefore Shep is a dog.

This is more difficult. Again the largest class is 'four-legged things' and 'dogs' and 'Shep' would fit inside that. But how do we know that 'Shep' would fit into the subclass of 'dogs', i.e. can we be certain that Shep is in fact a dog?

c) No dogs are birds. All sparrows are birds. Therefore no dogs are sparrows.

The first statement means that we draw two separate circles for the classes of 'dogs' and 'birds'. We put the subclass 'sparrows' as a smaller circle inside 'birds'. Ask the children if they would draw any other circles and if so what label(s) they would use.

d) Some old movies are black and white. Some magpies are black and white. Therefore some old movies are magpies.

Common sense tells us that while the two premises are valid, the conclusion is not. The outer circle would be labelled 'black and white things' with two smaller circles, 'some magpies' and 'some old movies' drawn inside it.

Incidentally, common sense can be defined as a basic ability to perceive, understand and judge things that are shared by – or common to – nearly everyone, and that can be agreed upon without further discussion. Having said that, common sense is by no means infallible. Things that seem to be so according to our common sense but which turn out not to be are 'counter-intuitive'. In science, for example, it's counter-intuitive that the Earth goes around the sun, when the evidence of our senses tells us that the Earth remains still and the sun moves around us. Similarly, warm water will freeze more quickly than cold water (the Mpemba Effect), whereas we would expect the opposite to be so as there is more heat-energy in warm water than in cold water. In philosophy, some thinkers argue that one's sense of the self as being permanent and unchanging (the idea of 'continuity of consciousness') is false. Julian Baggini, for instance, asserts that we are forever in flux, always moving from what we were through what we are now towards what we will become.[15]

Tip: You can help children understand the concept of counter-intuition by showing them optical tricks like this one – the well-known Müller-Lyer Illusion. Common sense tells us that the upper line is longer, whereas both lines are the same length.

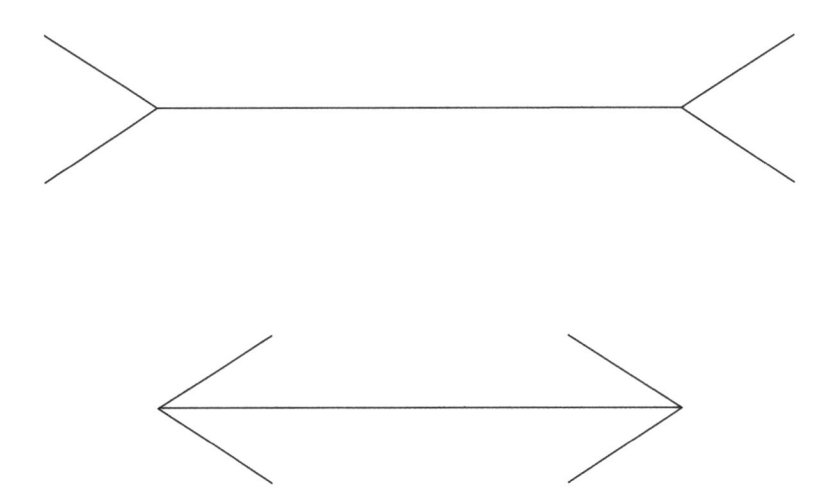

Figure 3.5

e) All children who have the latest smartphone will be accepted by the popular group. Ben has the latest smartphone. Therefore Ben will be accepted by the popular group.

The outer circle will be labelled 'owners of the latest smartphone'. Within that there will be a circle labelled 'people accepted by the popular group'. However, we cannot say for sure that *all* children with the latest smartphone will be accepted by the popular group, so there would need to be another circle labelled 'people not accepted by the popular group'. Given our uncertainty about the validity of the first proposition, we cannot place Ben inside either subclass – or we could place him in both with a question mark next to his name. Ask the children what they would label a circle placed around 'owners of the latest smartphone'.

AMBIGUITY

Ambiguity, or inexactness, occurs when something is open to more than one interpretation. One aim of a philosophical discussion is to clarify the meanings of words so that a shared understanding can be achieved.

Jumpstart critical thinking

Introduce the idea of ambiguity by showing the class some simple examples and ask:

- What are the two interpretations of each sentence?
- Which is the intended meaning in each case (where it's possible to decide)? Ask the children for the reasoning behind their choice.
- How could the sentences be reworded to make the intended meaning clear?

a) Any person not putting litter in this bin may be fined.
b) The town hall was built roughly 100 years ago.
c) The detective was as keen to catch the burglars as the police.
d) Steve slipped and almost broke his leg in several places on the icy pavement.
e) Tony told Alex that his missing cat had been found.
f) I saw a horse in the distance with my binoculars.
g) He fed her dog food.
h) Look at that pigeon with one eye.
i) I noticed the cup that Karl had won for running on the shelf.
j) Please wash your own cups and stand upside down on the draining board.

Take it further with some more difficult examples:

k) Exciting novels are rare. But rare books are expensive. Therefore exciting novels are expensive.

The ambiguity here lies in the two different ways in which the word 'rare' is used. In the first sentence it means that you do not come across exciting novels very often (even though there may be plenty of them around). In the second sentence it means that particular books of which only a small number exist are expensive for that reason.

l) Thank you for sending me a copy of your new book. I shall waste no time in reading it.

105

Here the ambiguity lies in the second sentence. It can either mean 'I will read your book immediately' or 'I will not read your book because to do so would be a waste of time'. This famous quote is attributed to various sources.

m) Then he remembered the picture of the film star he'd seen hanging in the cinema.

The ambiguity here lies in what the word 'hanging' refers to. Grammatically it refers to the film star, but common sense tells us that it was the picture he'd seen hanging.

n) In America a teenager gives birth once an hour.

The intended meaning is that in America girls in their teens collectively give birth once an hour, whereas the structure of the sentence suggests the meaning that just one teenager gives birth once an hour.

o) You could bring juice or water and a pudding to the picnic.

The sentence could be read as meaning that you could bring just juice to the picnic. Or it could mean you could bring water and a pudding to the picnic. Or it could mean that you could bring juice and a pudding to the picnic.

In philosophy ambiguity is not the same as vagueness. Here, vagueness is defined as a situation where there is no sharp dividing line between cases where a term applies and where it doesn't apply. So, for example, how much money you have in the bank makes you rich, or how many grains of sand make a heap are vague rather than ambiguous ideas.

Ambiguity also doesn't apply where people hold different views or theories about, for instance, being good. Here, 'good' isn't ambiguous but rather that there is some controversy over what the term means.

Moral ambiguity refers to a situation where the morally correct course of action isn't clear. A famous example is the lifeboat dilemma, where we are asked to imagine a lifeboat containing a number of people who have just abandoned a sinking ship. The lifeboat cannot take anyone else on board without capsizing and the freezing waters are infested with sharks. A man swims desperately towards the lifeboat and begs to be taken on board. What should the passengers do? (see Cohen 2003).

Tip: If you want the children to explore this issue, challenge them with slightly different scenarios. What if the person in the water was a young girl whose mother was already on board the lifeboat? What if one of the passengers was a man who had been convicted of murder, and everyone knew it? What if the person in the water had just discovered a cure for cancer and had been taking his research to a laboratory so that a trial drug could be created?

Incidentally, one of the most humane responses I have heard to this dilemma came from a Year 5 boy who thought that everyone should take turns of five minutes in the water. He said, 'They are all human beings and all deserve their chance to live.'

An important function of philosophy is to explore morally difficult topics, such as stem cell research, cloning, euthanasia and capital punishment in order to try to clarify and decide upon possible courses of action. (For a thorough and fascinating discussion of some ethical dilemmas, albeit from a Christian perspective, I highly recommend *Exploring Reality* by John Polkinghorne.)

SHIFT OF MEANING

Language is 'plastic' insofar as words drop out of use, new words come into existence, and words can change their meaning over time. In a philosophical discussion the idea of 'meaning shift' is subtler. What it means is that a term can change in the way it is used during the session, either inadvertently or deliberately. Thus, for example, we can say that 'Man is the only animal with self-awareness'. Here the use of the capital flags up the meaning of

'Man' as 'Mankind'. In a discussion, however, if that meaning is not made clear it could lead someone to think that only human males have self-awareness. Or take the statement, 'He's a good worker, and a man, so he's a good man.' Here the meaning of the word 'good' has shifted. First, it means hard-working or diligent, but when used a second time it means that 'goodness' is part of his character. A less clear-cut example concerns the use of the word 'laws' in science. Ordinarily we take a law to mean a set of rules within a society and understand that they were created by lawmakers. It would be a mistake to hold on unthinkingly to the implication that the 'laws' of Nature were therefore brought into existence by a cosmic Lawgiver. (If there is a God then of course He would have created the forces that allow the universe to exist as it does, but that's the subject of a different discussion.)

Ask the children if they can explain the shifts of meaning in the following sentences:

a) Rivers have banks, so the bank where I deposit my money is by a river.
b) The weather forecasts high winds, therefore we'll be fine here in the valley where we're low down not high up.
c) I have a right to read this book, therefore it's right for me to do that.
d) The sign says 'Fine for parking here', so it's perfectly fine for me to park here.
e) Religion teaches us to have faith as we pray. Faith is defined as an irrational belief. Therefore religion teaches us to be irrational.

SURFACE STRUCTURE AND DEEP STRUCTURE

'He tripped and fell over.' As I prepared to write this sentence I had a clear and detailed picture of the scene in my mind. In order to write it therefore, I left out much of the information that I was aware of at that moment. Furthermore, I consciously decided to leave out certain details but other omissions may have been subconsciously determined. The sentence itself makes sense and is grammatically correct, but it largely fails to communicate what was going on in my head. Also, if left unquestioned by others, different people will 'process' the sentence in various ways. Toby may have imagined an adult tripping over while Bhavna may have pictured a child. Sai may have based his imagined scenario on the memory of a real event, while Julia may have remembered a scene from a book she has read.

The difficulties are compounded during the flow of language between people talking together. During a discussion, for instance, the participants' thinking is happening quickly and, as they speak, the deletions and distortions of what is in their minds will be ongoing. In other words, what we say is just an approximation of what we are thinking, the tip of the mental iceberg as it were, and it is easy – maybe even inevitable – that listeners will take what limited information they hear and construct their own meanings that may bear little resemblance to the meaning the speaker intended to convey.

What we actually say is known as the surface structure of our thinking, based on the deep structure that is composed of all the thoughts we have about the topic or scenario in question. During a philosophical enquiry it's important that speakers think carefully about what meanings they want to convey, while listeners must be prepared to question what isn't clear rather than automatically 'joining the dots' in their minds and assuming the picture they come up with is the one that the speaker wanted them to have.

To help children develop this behaviour, read the following sentences one at a time. Ask the children to notice what they are picturing in their own heads and to note down some of the details. Afterwards, compare the different scenarios.

a) She walked into the shop with a smile on her face.
b) They made a brave attempt but failed in the end.
c) The cat walked along the wall then jumped down into the garden.
d) As it zoomed by the car went through a puddle and splashed the pedestrian.
e) Ten of them appeared without any warning.

Now show these next sentences to the class. What questions could the children ask to elicit more details and make the meanings clearer?

1. People should be allowed to decide for themselves.
2. It's a matter of opinion.
3. Mistakes were made but lessons were learned.
4. New Brillianto toothpaste is 50 per cent more effective.
5. I handled that situation badly.
6. Obviously he is better at that than the others.
7. Good teaching and learning are vital in a school.
8. You're smiling. Obviously you're enjoying the lesson.
9. You're not going to make up another excuse are you?
10. I know what you're thinking.

Commentary on these sentences:

1. This is our old friend the generalisation. Learn more by asking – Which people? Decide what for themselves? Why?
2. What is a matter of opinion? Is it entirely a matter of opinion? Is that always the case?
3. This is written in the personal impassive voice and the verbs 'made' and 'learned' are not specified. So we can reasonably ask – Who made the mistakes? What were the mistakes? Who learned the lessons and what were they?
4. There is an implied comparison here so the obvious question to ask is – The toothpaste is 50 per cent more effective than what? We might also ask what evidence the speaker has to justify that claim (and reject the vapid response, 'It's been clinically proven').
5. This is a (negative) judgement. To clarify its meaning we can ask what led the speaker to judge himself in this way.
6. Another judgement. First, we can question 'obvious' – Obvious to whom? We also need to know *what* he is better at than others and how that evaluation was made.
7. 'Teaching' and 'learning' are examples of what are called nominalizations, where verbs or processes have been turned into nouns or states (static things). While nominalizations are a useful 'shorthand' when communicating, they leave out the

essential dynamics of the processes being named. A useful analogy is to see a nominalization as one frame of a longer movie, a snapshot. Much information is lost when the 'action is frozen' (see also page 46). We can challenge statement 7 then by asking what essentially is involved in 'teaching' and 'learning' and by what standards these may be judged 'good'.
8. Here an assumption has been made that the lesson has caused the person to smile, which may not be the case. Clarify the situation by simply asking, 'What is making you smile?' and 'Are you enjoying the lesson?'
9. A presupposition is contained in the word 'another', in this case that the person being spoken to has made up excuses before.
10. This is the most obvious example of what's called 'mind reading', where one person assumes to know what's going on in another person's head. A simple solution is to 'catch yourself on' and realise that in the absence of sufficient (or any!) information you cannot know what another person is thinking.

As an aside, mind reading is also potentially harmful when it comes to issues of self-confidence. It is a negative habit of thinking and one that can go unnoticed so that eventually it 'runs in the background' and acts as a filter to the way a person perceives the world. So to think, 'He hasn't texted me for two days so he doesn't want to be my friend any more' is an example of mind reading that can be clarified by asking, 'Why haven't you texted me for two days?'

CRITERIA OF QUALITY IN A PHILOSOPHICAL ENQUIRY

In summing up some of the points touched on above, we can guide students towards a richer and more searching discussion by telling them explicitly about the criteria of quality they can try to build into what they say. These include questions and statements that:

- Give lots of information.
- Are relevant to the topic or idea being discussed.

- Add to what has already been said and move the discussion forward.
- Are open-ended, i.e. cannot be answered by a simple yes or no.
- Cannot be answered or resolved by looking things up in books or online.
- Are respectful towards the other people in the discussion.
- May be unexpected, i.e. embody creative connections between ideas.
- Are usually not easy to answer, i.e. call for further reflection.

The following is an extract from a sample discussion. Ask the children how they might alter some of what is being said to make the questions more powerful and the discussion richer and more focused.

Topic: Is it always right to punish another person for doing wrong?

1. If somebody does something bad then they should be punished. They have brought it on themselves.
2. But what if a person is mentally disturbed and didn't realise they were doing something wrong – it wouldn't be right to punish them then, would it?
3. No I suppose not. But let's say a mentally disturbed person was driving a car and injured a pedestrian. If you don't punish them, how will the injured person feel? After all, justice needs to be seen to be done. If crimes aren't punished then civilised society will crumble.
4. And what about little children? They need to be taught right from wrong and that can involve punishments as well as rewards. It's obvious isn't it?
5. I think that we're born knowing right from wrong. I think God gives us that knowledge when we come into the world.
6. Yes but if that's true, why doesn't *God* punish people when they do bad things?
7. Well that's a silly thing to say because you can't prove it. And what about if you don't believe in God?
8. Just because you don't believe in God doesn't mean that He doesn't exist ....

9. We could equally say that the idea of what's right and what's wrong comes from us, from people?
10. Wait a minute, I've had a thought. We've been talking about knowing that something might be right or wrong, but we have feelings about it too. If I see some kid being cruel to an animal, then I *feel* it's wrong. I might feel upset and angry and want to punish that kid. I wonder if the feelings come before the thought that what the kid is doing is wrong?
11. But maybe the kid is being cruel because he doesn't know any better. Or maybe people have been cruel to him so he thinks that's just normal behaviour. In his eyes he isn't doing anything wrong.
12. Then *he's* wrong. Any normal person would know that being cruel to animals is wrong.
13. What about fox-hunting though? Lots of people do that and don't think it's wrong.
14. Yes but if *most* people disapprove of fox-hunting and feel it's wrong, then we can say 'it's wrong'.
15. What if half of people thought that fox-hunting is right and half thought that it is wrong? Is it right or wrong then?
16. It depends on your point of view.
17. If you believe that, then somebody who murders a person out of revenge might believe he's doing the right thing ….
18. But the murderer would know in his heart that killing is wrong, no matter how angry he is. To me that proves that knowing right from wrong comes from God.
19. What if God changed his mind one day so that what was wrong yesterday is right today? We'd still know that, for example, murdering another person is wrong. Even if God disagreed, we'd still know what is *really* right and wrong.
20. I agree, because we can tell if someone's actions hurt another person. That's how we know right from wrong.
21. Yes but sometimes you've got to be cruel to be kind.

Commentary on the discussion
1. This is a vague generalisation. We could ask the speaker for examples, and consider any counter-examples. It would also be worth discussing if 'bad' and 'wrong' mean the same thing.

2. This is a useful counter-example, but the discussion could be enriched by turning the closed question into an open one – 'In what sense could we say it is wrong to punish a mentally disturbed person for doing something we think is bad?' There is also an opportunity here to explore the links between justice and morality.
3. We could make the point that justice amounts to more than punishment. It also involves understanding, mercy and forgiveness. We may also wonder whether the injured person would *inevitably* feel that punishment is called for.
4. Here we could consider the links between morality in a deeper sense and social conventions. If a little child pokes his tongue out at someone we could tell him that's being rude (in our culture). But is it 'wrong' in any other sense? If the child pokes his tongue out because he was copying his older brother, is he doing something wrong? Also, note the rhetorical question at the end of point 4.
5. This is a relevant point, though there is a danger here of the discussion losing focus. Summarising ideas about where morality might come from may be useful – from God/from ourselves/right and wrong as 'objective moral facts' independent of God or ourselves.
6. Here the discussion is moving off at a tangent. The point could be made that whether or not God exists, right and wrong exist in the world and the topic under consideration is whether it's *always* right to punish someone for doing wrong.
7. Here the facilitator could point out the disrespectful nature of the opening comment and bring the discussion back to the point of the topic.
8. Ditto here.
9. This point moves the discussion forward, though here we are now talking about the possible origins of morality rather than exploring whether it's always right to punish someone for doing wrong.
10. This touches on the so-called 'Feelings Theory' of morality, where we ourselves define things as being right or wrong depending on whether we approve or disapprove of someone's actions.

11. These points continue to explore the Feelings Theory and create the opportunity to discuss whether a sense of morality is relative and subjective or objectively existing 'out there' in an absolute sense. If there were only two people left in the world, Psi and Omega, and Omega murdered Psi for what he believed was a good reason, would Omega have done something wrong?
12. This opinion is not backed up by logical argument. We might also question what the speaker means by a 'normal' person.
13. This is a useful point that moves the discussion forward. There's an opportunity here also to explore what 'wrong' can mean in different contexts and to different degrees. For those who disapprove of fox-hunting, is it 'wrong' in the same sense that murder is wrong?
14. This point touches on the idea that wrongness 'comes from us' and is relative. If enough people believe that something is wrong (for whatever reason) does that make it truly wrong?
15. This usefully tests the idea of 'relative morality'.
16. This could be a 'thought stopper' (see page 45). It would be useful to wonder where a person's point of view comes from. If my point of view about a given situation comes about because I have blindly accepted what someone else has said, is it as acceptable or as sound as if I'd reasoned the matter out for myself? What if my blind acceptance of a viewpoint came from a respected authority in the field? What if my blind acceptance derived from my religious belief?
17. This is a useful example based on the if-then pattern of reasoning.
18. This supposition is unsupported and so goes no way towards substantiating the idea of God's existence.
19. 'What-if' is another useful tool in a philosophical discussion. This point challenges the assertion that morality comes from God. The word 'really' could also be challenged here. For example, does it refer to the notion that right and wrong are objective moral facts that are 'out there' anyway? And what does it mean to say 'out there'? If humans (or any sentient beings) didn't exist, would rightness and wrongness still exist in the universe?

20. We may wonder *how* we can tell someone's actions hurt another person. This point doesn't seem to take us forward. If we say we can tell when a person's actions hurt someone else, can we tell because morality comes from within ourselves (and how does that happen – genetics)? Or does morality come from God (another Big Philosophical Topic)? Or is morality just 'out there' (with the difficulties that idea raises, as in point 19)?
21. This is another potential thought stopper. In what sense has someone 'got to' be cruel to be kind? Does this imply that in certain situations the end justifies the means? What examples can we think of where this is so, and examples where it would not be justified?

Of course, the discussion doesn't end here, and indeed philosophers are still pondering where morality might come from, as the issue is by no means resolved. It is important for children to realise that the outcome of any enquiry may be more questions than they started with, or outright confusion, which causes us to realise that the issue is more complex and subtle than we originally thought.

KINDS OF QUESTIONS

As we will see in the next section, generating questions is a key feature of preparing for a philosophical enquiry and for deepening the discussion as it unfolds. Here are different kinds of questions you can encourage the children to ask.

The key or critical question
This is a question which opens up an issue based on one of the big ideas that philosophers like to explore. We will go into more detail on this later, but for now you can show the children one of the overarching themes and some key questions arising from it.

Freedom
- Is there such a thing as free will?
- Is it always better to have more choices?

- If God knows everything that you will do, can you truly have free will?

Happiness
- Should happiness be the most important thing in life?
- Do I have a right to be happy if it causes someone else to be unhappy?
- Would you rather be an unhappy human or a happy animal of your choice?

Consciousness
- Is my mind the same thing as my brain?
- How do thoughts cause my body to act, i.e. how can thought affect matter?
- Is my personality nothing more than my memories?

Reality
- What do we mean by 'real'?
- Can something be real for one person and not for another?
- Does real mean the same as true, as in true love?
- If life is a dream, does that matter?[16]

The branching question
This invites consideration of a choice between alternatives, supported by reasons for a decision. So, 'Would you rather save the life of a complete stranger, win a million pounds, read people's minds or live in good health to be a hundred?'

The divergent or open-ended question
This invites a range of responses from pupils, so – 'What do you think might happen if half of the people in the world suddenly doubled in height and so became more powerful?' Or 'In what ways is loyalty the same as friendship? In what ways do they differ?'

The inductive question
Here the answerer needs to give some examples in response to the question. So, 'How can you support your claim that human beings are basically kind?' 'If we say that something is unjust is that the

same as saying it is wrong? What situations support your view either way?'

The linking question
These are questions that take the discussion forward by building on previous questions. For example, 'You asked earlier if it was right to eat meat. If we could grow meat from stem cells, would that change your view, and if so how?'

Just as a matter of interest, in their SF book *The Space Merchants* (2003, first published in 1952), authors Frederick Pohl and Cyril Kornbluth write about Chicken Little, a huge mass of chicken meat grown in a vat for food. Apart from evoking a startling – and some would say horrifying – image, it illustrates the point that a great deal of science fiction wrestles with important philosophical issues. The children's author Douglas Hill said that all science fiction was predicated on the question 'what if?' and that good science fiction often took the form of a thought experiment that reflected back on the real world in significant ways (see 'Telling you something true' on page 26).

The reflective question
Questions like these are not expected to be answered immediately or off-the-cuff. They highlight the fact that thoughtful silences are an integral part of a philosophical discussion and are to be encouraged. It's perfectly reasonable for any child to ask for thinking time – and, I believe, in any lesson, not just a philosophical enquiry. Most if not all of the questions in the above categories could also be termed reflective questions.

The clarifying question
These questions help everyone in a discussion to crystallize their thoughts. So, 'Are you saying that ...?' 'Am I right in thinking ...?' 'Can you be more specific?'

The Big Six important questions
These are prefaced with who, what, where, when, why and how.

In their book *Asking Better Questions* (Morgan and Saxton 1994), the authors categorise the kinds of questions that form the basis of philosophical discussions as 'unanswerable' and refer to them as the eternal questions of existence. For children with an enquiring mind, this should be an exciting challenge encouraging further exploration, in the same way that many mountaineers want to climb Everest 'because it's there'.

As children take part in further philosophy sessions their questions are likely to become more refined and incisive. In the early days you must use your discretion in prompting children to look again at the questions they ask if they are not clear or are off the point. The only time when I would say you must intervene is if a child prefaces a question or statement with 'I know this may sound stupid but …'. My usual response to that is, 'How about – I know this will sound interesting, so …'.

Further to this, the SAPERE handbook for the Level 1 course offers the following useful categories:

- Information-processing questions where you ask for an explanation, more detail, an example, etc.
- Reasoning questions that seek evidence and reasons.
- Enquiry questions asking for connections and distinctions between ideas, and which challenge generalisations.
- Creative thinking questions that ask for speculation and 'thought experiments', and that seek to explore implications and the larger context.
- Evaluation questions checking for changes of mind, summaries, differences of view, conclusions, and what has been learned through the enquiry.

DIALOGUE REVISITED

Here are Phil and Sophy again having a short discussion about whether God exists. Ask the children to identify the kinds of questions being asked and if any of them could be improved.

Phil: I read the other day that the most basic question in philosophy is 'Why is there something rather than nothing?' (a)

Sophy: Well, one answer is that God made the universe.

Phil: Another answer, and one that many scientists believe, is that the universe came from nothing and that it was created by the Big Bang.

Sophy: But what caused the Big Bang?

Phil: I don't think we know the answer yet.

Sophy: By saying 'yet' you suggest that we will know the answer one day. But that is as much an act of faith as believing that God created the universe. Some people, including some scientists, believe that because the universe is 'just right' for life to begin – it's so finely tuned for life – that it couldn't have been a coincidence. (b)

Phil: It seems to me that having faith that science will explain how the Big Bang came about is just as reasonable as having faith in God. In fact it's *more* reasonable. We can see that the universe is expanding; all the galaxies are rushing away from each other. If we ran that backwards in time, we would see that all the galaxies would rush together and, at the start of time, clump into an incredibly tiny point. So there is strong evidence that the universe was created in the Big Bang ....

Sophy: So are you saying that either God created the universe or something – we don't know what – caused the Big Bang to happen? (c)

Phil: Yes, I suppose I am.

Sophy: But we could also reasonably say that God caused the Big Bang to happen, and that the Big Bang is itself evidence for God's existence.

Phil: I think we're going round in circles a bit.

Sophy: OK, fair enough. But I think we need to be clear that to ask 'Does God exist?' is not a scientific question. A scientific question is one that can be asked by forming a hypothesis (d) and testing it with experiments. If someone believes in God then you can't test his faith with experiments.

Phil: But his faith can be tested. What if this person's wife died in a car crash? His faith in God would be tested then, wouldn't it?

Sophy: Definitely, though we should consider whether we are giving the same meaning to the word 'faith' as a religious person does. But it's not being tested in the same way as a scientific hypothesis would be tested. Apart from that, millions and maybe billions of people have believed in God in one form or another for thousands of years. Surely all of those people couldn't be mistaken? (e)

Phil: Hundreds of years ago most people believed the Earth was flat, but they were wrong.

Sophy: Saying that lots of people were wrong in one way doesn't necessarily make them wrong in another way.

Phil: Point taken. But it does mean that lots of people can be wrong.

Sophy: But why do so many people feel the *need* to believe in God? Isn't that need itself evidence that God exists?

Phil: So you're saying that the *feeling* some people have that a Supreme Being exists suggests that such a being actually exists? (f)

Sophy: Yes. Don't we all like to think that life has some meaning?

Phil: I guess so. But let me get this right. Are you saying that the *feeling* of the need to believe is a *reason* to believe in God? (g)

Sophy: Are you saying that a feeling *doesn't* give you good reason to hold a belief?

Phil: Not exactly. But how can a feeling give you a good reason for doing or believing in something? (h)

Sophy: So, if a wife loves her husband she will trust him. The feeling of love is a reason to trust him.

Phil: But he might run away with another woman.

Sophy: That's beside the point. Her feeling of love is the basis of her reason for trusting him. If her trust ends up being betrayed, that's another matter.

Phil: What I don't get is that if God exists, why doesn't He make it obvious?

Sophy: What would be the benefit of making it obvious?

Phil: Well, we'd all know for sure!

Sophy: You're still thinking like a scientist. So if God suddenly appeared in the sky in a blaze of light and cured everyone who was sick and made evil vanish, you would count that as proof of His existence?

Phil: It would be hard not to count it as proof. Anyway, talking of science – in science there is a principle called Occam's razor, which says that the simplest explanation for something is the one that's most reasonable to accept (i). On that principle, the idea that there is just the universe is simpler than the idea that there is the universe plus God.

Sophy: I have three things to say about that. First, if the universe is *within* God, part of God, then we could say that ultimately there is just God. That's just as simple as saying there is just the universe. Second, some scientists talk about the 'multiverse' – an infinity of universes – as one way of explaining how our universe works. That is a much less simple explanation than saying there is 'just the universe' or there is 'the universe plus God'. Third, as far as I know there is no way for scientists to detect these other universes if they exist (j). So aren't we back to having faith in something than can't be proven?

Phil: The idea of the multiverse helps explain why our universe is as it is.

Sophy: I could equally say that the idea of God helps explain why our universe is as it is.

Phil: There's also the question of all the suffering in the world. If God is good, why doesn't He put a stop to that?

Sophy: Maybe He's allowing us to *choose* to be good (k) so that the end of suffering will come about by God working through people who have chosen that path.

Phil: What about the suffering that's not caused by wars and human evil? Things like earthquakes and disease and so on?

Sophy: If God exists and, through the creation of the universe, allowed us to exist and gave us intelligence, then by using our intelligence to find cures for disease and better ways of predicting earthquakes, He is still working His goodness through us. Don't you think that's a reasonable explanation? (l)

Phil: Hmm, I'll need to think about that.

Commentary on Phil and Sophy's discussion
a) For a concise discussion on this topic see Note 17 on page 154.
b) This is known as the Anthropic Principle. The 'weak' version states that the universe has developed in such a way that it can accommodate our existence (and the existence of life generally). The 'strong' version may be summed up by saying, 'somehow the universe knew we were coming' (attributed to the physicist Freeman Dyson).

c) This is a clarifying question. Another option that may be considered with regard to the existence of the universe is that it's a 'brute fact' – it just *is*. For me this viewpoint is highly unsatisfying.
d) A hypothesis is a possible explanation based on observed phenomena. A theory is more robust, namely an explanation based on a strong body of evidence and/or well-verified or proven facts.
e) This question embodies the 'appeal to the people' (*ad populum*) tactic in a discussion (see page 92). Note also the rhetorical use of the word 'surely'.
f) This is a clarifying question. Phil is restating what Sophy said to be sure that he understands her point.
g) Another clarifying question. There would also be an opportunity here to discuss how a feeling (intuition, gut instinct, etc.) could count as evidence, or a reason to feel that something is true.
h) This is a 'procedural how question' asking for information about how something is done or can be so. Other how questions relate to quantity (how much/how many), quality (relating to the senses – how does it look, feel, sound, etc.) and extent (how convinced are you that …, etc.).
i) Occam's razor is attributed to the Franciscan friar William of Ockham (*c.* 1287–1347), who said that 'entities should not be multiplied unnecessarily'. That is to say that among a number of competing hypotheses it is reasonable to select the one that makes the fewest assumptions. The principle is also known as the 'law of parsimony'.
j) The multiple universe or 'bubble universe' hypothesis says that every choice we make causes a split or branching of reality so that every possible option is played out somewhere. The multiverse idea can offer an explanation as to why our universe is so 'fine tuned' to allow consciousness to exist, insofar that given an infinite number of universes, at least one will inevitably allow human life to evolve – and we just happen to be in it. Despite what Sophy says, other sources argue that there is some evidence that parallel universes exist.[18]
k) This is the 'free-will argument'; the notion that in the realm of space-time people are free to make choices. Although some philosophers argue that free will doesn't exist (for example,

that we are ultimately controlled by our genes), it does support the idea that indeterminacy in the universe allows for the presence of true creativity. This in itself is a topic that can form the basis of a rich philosophical enquiry. See also Polkinghorne (2005) for an in-depth exploration of this topic.
l) This is a reflective question, and one that Phil is wise to want to think about further.

SO WHAT IS A PHILOSOPHICAL QUESTION?

Philosophical questions are questions that can be examined and explored through questioning and logical reasoning. They cannot be answered by scientific investigation, although scientific ideas and facts can form part of a discussion involving philosophical questions. Often philosophical discussions are about big ideas such as truth, reality, good and evil, morality, God, identity and knowledge – although this is not invariably so. What's important is that the aim of an enquiry is to generate insights and further understanding to help people lead richer and more fulfilling lives.

EMBEDDED ASSUMPTIONS

An assumption is something that is accepted without proof, in the form of facts and/or reasoned argument. Phil and Sophy in their discussion above are challenging one another's ideas as far as they can through reasoned argument. Phil, for example, may believe that God does not exist, but he doesn't assume so: he is putting forward arguments that support his belief while testing Sophy's arguments that God may exist (though again she is not assuming that He does). One aim of philosophical discussion is to highlight assumptions and test them. Some assumptions people make are 'embedded', which is to say that they form part of a belief system but are 'hidden'; unrecognised and therefore untested. So, for instance, Phil may argue that one weakness of religious faith is unquestioning belief in Scripture, where embedded assumptions exist that the universe was intentionally created by a Supreme Being who involves Himself in human affairs and has revealed His presence and His plan to people. Sophy may argue that Phil's faith in science is built on the hidden assumption that science will eventually be able to answer all questions about the universe, including a (materialistic) explanation of why some people have faith in God.

Here are some examples where embedded assumptions may lead to false conclusions. Ask the children how they can explain these puzzles.

a) Inspector Corner of Scotland Yard and his men were searching the snow-clad moors for escaped convict Phil Bowman. Just as they were about to give up, one of the officers spotted a body. Bowman was found lying dead in the snow. There were no tracks leading to or from the body. The cause of death was partially due to the unopened pack on his back. Bowman did not die of thirst, hunger or cold. What was in Bowman's pack that led to his death?

Answer: An unopened parachute. The false embedded assumption was that Bowman's pack was a backpack, not a parachute pack. In addition, some will have assumed that he arrived on the moors somehow by land, not by air.

b) Romeo and Juliet are dead. The room in which the bodies lie is locked from the outside. Opposite the door are French windows that are partly open. Long, heavy drapes are partially drawn across. Near the windows is a small table. On the floor near the table there is broken glass and liquid on the carpet among the shards.

Tip: Turn this into a game of 20 questions. Most children will falsely assume that Romeo and Juliet are people, whereas in fact they are goldfish.

c) Two train tracks run parallel with one another for their entire length, except where they join to form a single track over the Farsight Bridge, which gives a splendid view across the valley. One afternoon train heading south speeds on to the bridge.

A second train heading north speeds on to the bridge. Neither train can stop on the short bridge. What happens?

Children who say that the trains crash have made the false assumption that the trains reached their ends of the bridge at the same time, whereas in fact their journeys took place at different times in the afternoon.

CONTRADICTIONS

A contradiction occurs where one or more statements are in opposition to each other. In logic the law of non-contradiction says that statement S and not-S cannot both be true. Some logical contradictions are easy to spot:

a) The tiny giant.
b) A gentle torturer.
c) It's my only choice.
d) I have an original copy of the picture.
e) The time is approximately 4.32 and 20 seconds.
f) Romeo is married to Juliet but Juliet is not married to Romeo.
g) God is all-powerful, so He can create a rock that is too heavy for Him to lift.

Other statements seem at first to be contradictory but may have logical explanations. Ask the children if they can come up with any for these:

h) A snowy August afternoon. (I could be standing on top of a snow-capped mountain at the time.)
i) Tony was rich and homeless. (Tony's riches might be a feeling of freedom and the fact that all of his time was his own.)
j) He offered her another biscuit for the first time. (He offered her a custard cream, which she refused, then offered her a jammy dodger, the first time he had done so, which she accepted.)
k) I love you and I hate you. (In a complex relationship, extremes of feeling are possible.)

Jumpstart critical thinking

l) My younger brother is the only child in our house. (The speaker may no longer live in the house, or may now be an adult.)
m) The restaurant opens at five o'clock and it begins serving food between four and nine. (The restaurant might open at five in the morning but serve only drinks until four in the afternoon, when food also begins to be served.)

Contradictions also crop up in proverbs. Ask the children to match up the contradictory pairs from these two lists:

1. All good things come to those who wait.
2. The best things in life are free.
3. You're never too old to learn.
4. Absence makes the heart grow fonder.
5. Too many cooks spoil the broth.
6. You can't teach an old dog new tricks.
7. Many hands make light work.
8. Time and tide wait for no one.
9. There's no such thing as a free lunch.
10. Out of sight, out of mind.

Answers: 1–8, 2–9, 3–6, 4–10, 5–7.

Now ask the children if they can resolve the contradictions in any of the pairs. For instance, looking at 2 and 9 we might say that a lunch is not one of the best things in life.

In a discussion, highlighting any contradictions that occur creates the opportunity for children to restate what they mean more clearly. In life generally, contradictory behaviour is quite common:

- A law-abiding person is fined for speeding several times but does not change the way he drives.
- Some people download pirated software, music and films but would never think of stealing from a shop.
- Phil gets upset watching advertisements asking for money for charities but never makes a donation.

Contradictions, whether true or apparent, can form the basis for some interesting discussions. For example:

- Is it wrong for an animal lover to eat meat?
- Can a female want to look pretty by wearing make-up, etc. and argue for feminism?
- Is it right for a parent to say to a child, 'Do as I say not as I do'?
- Is it acceptable to judge others for bad things we do ourselves?
- Is it reasonable for someone to want tougher controls on immigration yet will happily buy goods made by immigrants who are on very low wages?

MORAL DILEMMAS

A moral dilemma is a situation in which there is a conflict between two or more courses of action where each course of action would bring some benefit or good. We have already looked at examples (see pages 20 and 105). Choosing any course of action is therefore undesirable insofar as not choosing the other courses may bring harm.

Moral philosophy is that branch of philosophy concerned with ideas of what is good or bad, with the practical intention of how we should best live our lives. Discussing moral dilemmas in the classroom confronts children with difficult situations that allow them to reflect on their own values and beliefs, what they should do, what they would do and why. As with most philosophical discussions, tackling moral dilemmas requires creative and critical thinking and a degree of empathy.

Chapter 4 takes you through the process of setting up a community of enquiry in the classroom, where various moral dilemmas can be more fully explored. For now we will touch upon some well-known examples.

a) You find a wallet containing £100 pounds on the pavement. No one else is around and there are no clues in the wallet as to the owner. What do you do?

Jumpstart critical thinking

Ask the children to think about what they would personally do and what they think they ought to do, if the two courses of action are different. What if the wallet contained £500? What if the wallet had an address inside? What if the wallet contained £100 and the name and address of your enemy? If the wallet contained a photograph of an elderly person, would that cause you to choose a different course of action? If the wallet contained a photograph of a man in an expensive suit standing beside a top-of-the-range BMW, would you choose a different course of action?

What other scenarios can you think of?

b) Society should always operate on the principle of the greatest good for the greatest number.

In other words, society should always be governed so that the majority of people benefit, even if it means that some minorities do not. How strongly do you agree or disagree with this idea?

What if the government had only enough money to offer healthcare to people over the age of 60, who (for the sake of argument) formed the majority of the population? How do you feel about that?

What if the government only had enough money to provide free education up to the end of Year 6 and after that parents would have to pay for their children to go to school? Would you want your parents to pay? (This is not about whether or not you like school, but whether you want to gain qualifications for a reasonable job.)

What if the government could allocate a pot of money to only one of the following groups? Which would you choose and why?

1. Pensioners.
2. People earning less than the living wage.
3. People who are in debt through no fault of their own.
4. People needing constant medical care at home.
5. A group of your choice.

Note: 'The greatest good for the greatest number' is the principle of utilitarianism, espoused by the philosopher and social reformer Jeremy Bentham (1748–1832).

c) Your friend gives you the money to buy him a lottery ticket just before he goes on holiday. You spend your own pocket-money buying yourself a ticket too. One of the tickets wins a jackpot of £10,000. Your friend returns from holiday and asks how he did in the lottery.

- What options could you choose?
- What option do you choose and why?

d) Before your teacher arrives to take the register, someone in class throws a tennis ball and smashes a glass ornament on the teacher's desk. Your teacher wants to know who did it. Would you tell?

- Would you tell if it was your best friend?
- Would you tell if the culprit was your enemy?
- Would you tell if you neither liked nor disliked the culprit?
- Would you change your mind if your best friend threw the ball and the teacher threatened to keep the whole class in every break time for a week if someone didn't tell?

e) Imagine that a huge asteroid is going to strike the Earth in ten years' time and wipe out civilisation. In your country the government orders the building of a spaceship that can carry 100 people and all they'll need to establish a colony on Mars.

- What groups of people do you think should be allowed to go? (By groups, you may choose certain professions, certain age groups, etc.).
- Are there any particular groups in society that you think should definitely *not* be allowed to go?
- Are there any particular people who should be allowed to go? (These might be people you actually know, celebrities, etc.).
- Are there any particular people who should definitely *not* be allowed to go and why?

CHAPTER 4
Jumpstart a community of enquiry

Philosophical discussion sessions follow a certain protocol; a number of stages that build up to the enquiry proper, incorporating what Matthew Lipman (see page xi) calls 'the spirit of enquiry', the ethos or attitude of all participants as they explore each others' ideas.

PERSONAL PREPARATION

The books I've noted in the References were of particular help to me when I started to explore the idea of doing philosophy in the classroom. There are scores of other publications, plus many free resources online, including some excellent filmed sessions and talks available on YouTube and www.ted.com/. In conjunction with these, I would recommend going on a couple of courses. I studied with SAPERE which offer thorough training and useful support materials. You may also find that there are other P4C schools in your area which have already formed, or would be willing to form, a network for sharing ideas and resources. The network I belonged to held occasional in-person meetings, but much of the interaction happened via email, so the time commitment wasn't onerous.

Ideally your whole school, management and colleagues, will want to go down the P4C route and build regular enquiry sessions into the curriculum. The educational benefits are now beyond dispute – search online for dozens of articles, research studies and anecdotal evidence that will amply justify the time and effort involved.

If however you are a 'lone candle in the dark' then I encourage you to persevere, perhaps by setting up a lunchtime philosophy club. It won't be long before the children who attend spread the word to teachers and classmates about the fun of doing philosophy and how it is helping them in other areas of learning.

If you have yet to launch your first philosophy session then my advice is simply to relax and enjoy it. The complexities of running enquiries mean that most probably nobody gets it all right first time round. A community of enquiry evolves over time, and that includes the confidence and expertise of the facilitator. As a first step, let the children do the thinking work while you guide them with a light touch (see 'The role of the facilitator' on page 145).

SETTING UP THE SPACE

Ideally, you and the children should sit in a circle. Explain that this is for the same reason King Arthur had a round table, because everyone's ideas are equally valued and welcome. Remind the children about the spirit of the enquiry, which includes active and attentive listening, respect for others, and careful consideration of the ideas being expressed. Emphasise that an enquiry is not an argument – the aim is not to win but to explore ideas collaboratively to reach a greater understanding of the issues being discussed.

Time constraints mean that the enquiry may not have run its natural course and with no conclusions having been reached. As far as possible allow time towards the end to help the children summarise the main points covered and what has been learned or concluded so far. It may be that you can continue exploring the same topic in the next session. Supplying every child with a 'thinking journal' means that they can record and revisit what they got out of the sessions. Encourage the children also to note down any meaty questions they would like to discuss in future, plus quotes and other snippets they find of interest. You might also create a 'Philosophy Board' for the same purpose.

GETTING READY TO THINK

As an introduction to the session proper you can spend a few minutes on 'mind warm-ups' with the class. You'll find a number of these in this book, or search online. Some colleagues prefer more physical teamwork games, though if the children seem to have an excess of energy or are highly excitable after a PE or games lesson, for example, then opt for a 'settling down' technique instead.

Controlled breathing
Ask the children to sit relaxed on their chairs with hands resting in their laps. Eyes can be open or closed, though if open children can stare at a point on the wall and not distract themselves by looking around the room. Ask them to become aware of the position of their bodies and to notice the weight of their bodies on the chair. Get them to breathe normally for 30 seconds or so (ideally through the nose), then exhale slowly and fully for a slow count of four; then inhale fully and slowly to a slow count of four; hold the breath for a count of four, then repeat the pattern another three or four times.

The listening game
Ask the children to sit quietly. Tell them that all you want them to do is listen. You might ask them to notice as many sounds in the room and around the school as they can. Notice far away sounds, nearby sounds (such as their own breathing), high sounds, low sounds, etc. Use various materials to make different sounds: the crackle of cellophane, the tap of a pencil on a tabletop, the tinkling of a small bell. Invite the children to bring in objects that make interesting sounds (within reason!).

Visualisation
Tell the children to settle themselves down as above, again leaving the choice to them as to whether they want to keep their eyes open or closed. The visualisation itself might be a simple description of a calming scene, though mention what it will be beforehand so that any children can opt out if they wish. This is an important point. If you intend to describe a beach scene, for example, and a child in your class was once nearly washed out to sea and drowned, his visualisation may be anything but calming.

One of my favourite visualisations is to imagine a tennis ball floating in the air. Set it spinning one way, then another. Make it change colour. Now make it rainbow coloured. Enlarge it, shrink it, transform it into a soap bubble, then back into a tennis ball, before –magically – making it turn inside out with a loud rubbery pop.

Another technique is to play an extract of calming music or nature sounds such as a gentle breeze or a quietly flowing stream. Copyright-free downloads or streamed extracts are plentiful online.

STIMULUS

As you and the children become more experienced enquirers, you will find that just about anything can serve as a stimulus for launching a discussion session. Pictures, picture books, poems, comics, news articles, video clips, an object, extracts from stories or non-fiction books, topics the children are studying – all of these are rich sources of ideas for enquiries. In his useful *Pocket P4C* Jason Buckley (The Philosophy Man) recommends using stimuli that raise one or more big ideas (see page 34), highlight opposite notions such as wealth and poverty, or subtle distinctions such as lying and pretending.

THINKING TIME

Once the stimulus has been presented, give the children time to think about and discuss it individually or in groups: thinking journals may be used to record first thoughts, feelings and questions. If the children are not used to this yet, try using the 'mini-think' technique at the warm-up stage.

Mini-think
Prepare some cards, each featuring a simple image. You can show a card to the whole class and ask for responses – questions, first thoughts, opinions. Alternatively, split the class into groups, give each group a set of cards and ask for these cards to be turned over one at a time at random. The aim is to make creative links between

Jumpstart a community of enquiry

Figure 4.1
Source: Tony Hitchman

the cards or simply keep up a running commentary about them as thoughts come to mind. For example:

- 'I wish I had a spell to make money appear!'
- 'What does "magic" mean?'
- 'If you wish for something hard enough, can it ever come true?'
- 'Is wishing the same as praying?'
- 'If everyone could do magic, how would the world be different?'
- 'You'd have magic criminals and magic police!'
- 'Is the word "spell" in magic linked to the idea of spelling a word?'
- 'Are miracles in the Bible examples of magic?'

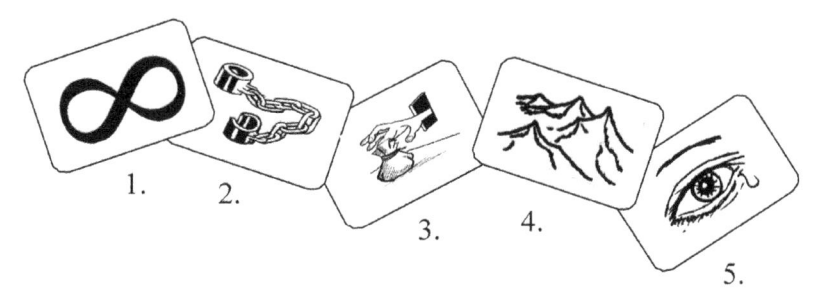

Figure 4.2
Source: Tony Hitchman

1.
- 'In maths this means infinity.'
- 'You could keep going round and round forever.'
- 'Is forever a real thing though or just an idea?'

135

- 'The universe must end sometime.'
- 'Would you want to live forever?'

2.
- 'Shackles. Doing time in prison.'
- 'Is prison the best way to deal with criminals?'
- 'What if you could magically take time from criminals' lives?'
- 'Like, make them age five years or ten or whatever in a second?'
- 'Spending time in prison is part of the punishment.'
- 'Some criminals in prison study or learn a trade and try to be better people.'
- 'Some just stay bad when they get out.'

3.
- 'If my family was starving and I stole food, would that be wrong?'
- 'Would it be more wrong to steal money?'
- 'That's what justice is for, to decide how wrong something is.'
- 'What if you could magically steal time off other people and use it yourself?'
- 'What if everyone could do that – it would be a horrible world!'
- 'Can it ever be right to steal something?'

4.
- 'What have mountains got to do with stealing?'
- 'Mountains last a long time, but not forever.'
- 'Time is more powerful than stone.'
- 'You need to be strong and determined to climb mountains.'
- 'Maybe it's the same if you've done wrong but want to be good again.'
- 'But if you're just forgiven, that doesn't mean you need to be strong and determined.'
- 'Even if you're forgiven by someone, you can still feel guilty inside.'
- 'If you do your time in prison for a crime, are you still guilty when you come out?'

5.
- 'If you feel bad, I mean upset, after doing wrong does that make you less of a criminal?'
- 'Why are there bad feelings in the world, like being upset or angry or jealous?'
- 'That's just the way things are.'
- 'It's like saying, why do bad things happen in the world?'
- 'If there is a God, why does He allow people to have bad feelings?'
- 'If there were only good feelings, how would you know they were good?'
- 'So do you mean we *need* bad feelings to know what good feelings are?'

Mini-thinks are not philosophical enquiries on a small scale. They are intended to get the creative juices flowing and also help lessen inhibitions children may have about offering their ideas to the 'collective pool'. As you see, they can also throw up connections and questions that would make rich and interesting topics for later, full-blown philosophical discussions.

What's important is that children are given some know-how about what to do in their thinking time. The mini-think is one idea, but you could instruct the children in other ways. Use the image in Figure 4.3 as an example stimulus.

- What are your first thoughts as you look at this picture?
- What feelings did you experience?
- How do you think this child is feeling?
- What questions could you ask about this picture?
- What questions does the picture suggest in a more general way?
- Summarise this child's situation in one sentence.

Note that children don't necessarily need to be articulating their thoughts in groups. Thinking time can be an individual period of silent reflection. Thoughts can be noted in thinking journals, connected as a mind map, turned into a short description, poem or story extract, or sketched out in cartoon form. Afterwards you may want children to pair up with classmates and share their ideas.

Figure 4.3
Source: Tony Hitchman

QUESTION MAKING

> Out of clutter, find simplicity.
>
> Albert Einstein

The next stage of the enquiry process is to take the material that the children have already generated and from it create a number of meaty philosophical questions, ideally ones that are of interest to everyone and have some practical value in the children's lives. Philosophical questions are ones that are open to collaborative, informed and rational examination; that can accommodate (respectful) disagreement and further questioning; and that cannot be answered only through scientific investigation and so-called 'sense experience', i.e. what each of us subjectively perceives. (Interestingly, though empiricism is a stance in philosophy which asserts that *all* knowledge comes only from sensory experience; although within the philosophy of science it includes evidence that may be derived from experiments.)

Furthermore, philosophical questions invite rich discussion, can accommodate a range of different opinions that can be supported by examples, and may lead, not necessarily to any firm conclusion, but to a raft of other questions and opportunities for further enquiry. Examples include the following:

- Is my mind the same as my brain?
- Is it wrong to buy luxuries when millions of people in the world are starving?
- Should criminals have the same human rights as everyone else?
- Am I the same person I was five years ago?
- Would you choose to live in a computer simulation if you were happier there?
- Do we avoid committing crimes just because we fear being caught?
- Are the best things in life free?
- Do we have souls?
- How can people believe that something is true without evidence?
- What is education?

If the children are having difficulty creating the kinds of questions that would make for a rich enquiry, prompt and guide as necessary but if possible avoid spoon-feeding the class with your own ideas. One way of helping children along is to look for the concepts behind their questions; more philosophically based questions can then grow out of these.

1. Why do we have to learn maths at school?
Themes include learning, maths, schools.

- Were numbers invented or discovered by humans?
- What does it mean to have learned something?

- If there were no humans, would numbers exist?
- What is knowledge?
- How do we know that we know something?

2. Why do people speak different languages?

Themes include language, intelligence, communication.

- Without language, would thoughts be possible?
- Are thoughts real things?
- Could people communicate clearly without language?
- Can we call the sounds that whales and dolphins make language?
- What does intelligence mean?

3. Why do I get upset sometimes?

Themes include feelings, relationships, being human.

- What is a feeling?
- Can a feeling be called a fact?
- How are thoughts and feelings linked?
- Is it possible for a person to have no feelings?
- Do animals have feelings?
- Would an artificially intelligent computer have feelings?
- If I feel upset and my friend feels upset, are we both feeling the same thing?

AIRING AND SHARING THE QUESTIONS

Since valuing children's thinking is an important part of a community of enquiry, it's only fair that everyone's questions should be looked at before one question is chosen for discussion. The various stages of preparing for an enquiry do not need to be done all at once. Presenting the stimulus, thinking time and generating questions can happen on a different day to airing-and-sharing and choosing which question will be discussed; though subsequent stages of the enquiry process are best done in one session.

Tip: Create a 'treasure box of thoughts' for the questions that are not chosen and use these from time to time as the basis for further enquiries. This is another way of allowing the children to know that their ideas are valued and also means that you won't have to find a different stimulus for every discussion.

Help the children to have an informed vote on which question will be discussed by:

- Asking if any of the questions can be answered without the need for a philosophical discussion. Can the answers be found in a book or by an Internet search, for instance?
- Checking to see whether any of the questions can be amalgamated, or whether two or more questions are very similar.
- Inviting the child or group who created the question to explain why it would make for an interesting discussion.
- Asking the class to consider whether a given question is important and may lead to insights that will be of practical value.
- Seeing whether the question can generate further questions.

CHOOSING WHICH QUESTION TO DISCUSS

This is usually done by voting, which can take a number of forms. My own preference is the so-called 'mole vote'. Here all the questions are read out without any vote being taken, then the children close their eyes and do a thumbs-up or put up a hand for their chosen question as they are read out slowly again. Keeping eyes closed means that the children don't just vote with their friends.

Another popular voting method is to write down the questions on large sheets of paper. Lay these on the floor, set a time limit of several minutes, ask the children to look at all the questions, then to stand by the one they would like to discuss. An advantage of this method is that the children can change their minds before the time limit is up. You can allow the children more than one vote, but they can use only one of them to vote for their *own* question. If you want the children to vote with their feet in this way, give each child counters for the number of votes they are allowed and tell them to put these on the question sheets of their choice.

FIRST THOUGHTS

Giving children a few minutes to chat more informally about the chosen question allows thoughts to be arranged and clarified, and for strong views to be expressed at the outset (with the expectation that once this 'emotional charge' has been released, opinions can be articulated in a more considered way during the enquiry proper). This time also accommodates 'first snatched thought syndrome', where children may respond with a mental knee-jerk reflex; an opinion perhaps picked up from someone else and not one that they have thought through for themselves.

First thoughts time can also be used for the group whose question was chosen to explain how they came to decide on it, though this may have been done at the airing-and-sharing stage.

BUILDING: THE CORE OF THE ENQUIRY

This is the meat of the enquiry, where philosophical tactics or 'moves' (see below) are used to explore the question as thoroughly as possible in the time available. Remind the children of the etiquette you expect from them: of listening carefully, not interrupting, being patient and respecting the views of others. Note also these points of procedure:

As far as possible do not lead or dominate the enquiry. The 'locus of control' should shift to the children. You are one enquirer among many. However, intervene if the discussion becomes a simple swapping of opinions and anecdotes, or if the enquiry seems to be grinding to a halt. Use the same tactics you want the children to learn as a way of refreshing and refocusing things:

- Restate the last comment made to be sure that everyone understands.
- Ask for a reason or example, or ask a further question.
- Refer back to an earlier part of the dialogue.
- Make a creative link between two or more ideas (or invite the children to do this).

- Provoke disagreement by offering a contrary view.
- Take a brief time-out with a thinking game.
- Summarise the dialogue so far.

- Children who want to contribute can indicate this by holding out a hand palm up rather than the usual hand up in the air. This highlights the difference between an enquiry and a conventional lesson, and signifies that the children are being 'open handed' with their thoughts and the time they spend listening to the viewpoints of their classmates.
- Try to include everyone in the discussion. Do not force anyone to speak, but say from time to time, 'Is there anyone who hasn't spoken yet who'd like to offer their thoughts?' As the facilitator, point out people who have been waiting a long time to speak but as far as possible let each speaker choose the next.
- Encourage children to be as succinct as possible. Some children may ramble (and some just like the sound of their own voice!). While this tendency will probably fade over time, indicate to a child whose contribution is long-winded to come to the point. I prefer to angle my hands with fingertips touching as a visual signal to indicate this, rather than verbally interrupting the child who's speaking. Some children will try to dominate the dialogue by wanting to speak often. One way of preventing this is to give such a child five or six counters and explain, 'You obviously have lots of good ideas to offer, but we only have a limited time in the session. So I want you to think about which thoughts you want us all to hear – the very best ones – and spend a token each time you'd like to speak.' I've found that children who ramble or try to dominate are not picked as often to speak by their classmates, so doing something to change these behaviours early on in the evolution of the community will bring benefits in the long run.

LAST THOUGHTS

Allow time towards the end of the session to help children sum up what has been learned, what conclusions have been drawn and what further questions have come out of the discussion. It's rare that you will all reach a consensus on an issue: let the children talk in pairs or groups and then, again succinctly, present their conclusions or further questions to the class.

As a follow-up to this, get each child to write their opinion or a question or other idea on a sticky note and make a display of these as an *aide-mémoire* of the session. Encourage the children to write about the session in their thinking journals and to talk about it with family and friends.

REVIEW

Evaluating each session helps the community to evolve. Ways of doing this include asking:

- What really worked well? What didn't work so well and why?
- How could we make the next session better?
- What 'moves' really helped the enquiry along? You can prepare for this by giving the children a skills checklist and asking them to make a tally mark each time they use a philosophical tactic. A variation of this is to create 'skills buddies', pairs of children who monitor each other during a session and note the moves they make.
- How can we use what we learned in our lives more generally?

You may also want to video the session and review it with the class later, in order to ask the above questions. Keeping your own personal diary of how things went, together with tips you pick up from others, from books, online, etc. is also very useful.

It is important to realise that it takes time for a community to evolve and for children to master the range of skills needed to take part in a rich and fruitful enquiry. The educator Will Ord advises, 'by increments conquer' or we might say, how do you eat an elephant? One little bit at a time.

THE ROLE OF THE FACILITATOR

We have touched on some of the functions of the facilitator above. The word 'facilitate' comes from the Middle French meaning 'easy' and, earlier, from the Latin *facilis* meaning 'easy to do'. While you may not think that doing philosophy with the children is easy, especially in the early stages, we might best regard the general role of the facilitator as 'easing the way' for the community to grow. Initially you will be the facilitator, but, as we have seen, one aspect of your role is to 'relinquish control' to the children so that eventually they will sustain the community and eventually take it in turns to facilitate enquiries themselves.

More specifically, the facilitator's role is to:

- Explain the benefits of doing philosophy (see my Introduction and Afterword).
- Establish the classroom ethos within which enquiries are undertaken. As we have seen, this includes respectful, attentive listening, patience, tolerance, and playfulness with and yet rigorous assessment of ideas.
- Establish the procedure for conducting an enquiry.
- Make the skills explicit. If a child, for instance, offers a counter-example, let him or her and the whole class know.
- Intervene as necessary but with a light touch if the discussion slows or begins to turn into a mere debate or exchange of opinions (without supporting reasons).

SKILLS CHECKLIST

Help children to become confident in using these skills by:

- Making them explicit in an enquiry; in other words, when a child offers an example, point that out and give credit for doing it.
- Model the behaviour. Display those skills yourself. This will not only make them clearer for the children but allow them to realise that 'it's OK for us to be like that too'.

- Monitor the skills in the children and/or have them do it for themselves.
- Encourage the same skills in the children's learning more generally.

Skills to be encouraged are:

- Respectful listening. Listening with interest and without interrupting.
- Suggesting and sharing ideas. This is an important aspect of a *community* of enquiry, where possessiveness ('That was my idea') is discouraged.
- Expressing ideas clearly and succinctly, which includes choosing words carefully.
- Building on or expanding the ideas others give.
- Reasoning. Giving reasons for opinions and offering reasoned arguments.
- Defining. Asking for clarification of a term and/or restating it in your own words (clarifying and restating are also key skills).
- Questioning – which includes asking a question about a question.
- Searching for and evaluating evidence.
- Making distinctions between terms, concepts and arguments.
- Offering examples and counter-examples.
- Connecting. Making creative links between ideas.
- Speculating, for instance, about the consequences of an action or situation.
- Spotting contradictions between viewpoints.
- Generalising – 'So does this apply in every case?' – but also being wary of generalisations (see page 55).
- Summarising. Summing up the argument so far, what has been learned, etc.

Note that most of these items are the philosophical 'moves' or tactics mentioned elsewhere for deepening an enquiry, moving it forward and testing for truth.

SAMPLE DIALOGUE

Here's an extract from a dialogue between a small group of Year 5 and Year 6 children around the question 'What is courage?' Ask the class to identify the various philosophical skills/moves being shown. You may find that your own children get drawn into the discussion – challenge them further by testing what Faisal and his friends are saying against quotes on the theme of courage that are readily available online.[19]

1. Facilitator: So the question is, 'What is courage?'
2. Faisal: Maybe you've heard this sentence, 'Feel the fear and do it anyway.' I think if you do something you're frightened of doing then you're being courageous.
3. Lauryn: I looked the word up earlier and a synonym for courage is fearlessness. If you're fearless it means you have no fear. So doesn't that contradict what you've just said?
4. Faisal: It does when you put it like that.
5. Hailey: So I wonder if courage isn't just one thing. Can you have courage when you do something you're frightened of doing, and a different kind of courage when you're fearless?
6. Kian: I agree with Hailey that just to call the whole thing we're talking about 'courage' is a bit too simple. And going on from what you said Hailey; can you be just a little bit courageous? I mean, if I was just a bit nervous about doing something but did it anyway, that wouldn't be as courageous as doing something I was terrified about, but still went ahead with it.
7. Facilitator: Bearing all these things in mind, I wonder then if we can talk about *degrees* of courage and *contexts* of courage?
8. Eve: Do you mean being courageous in different situations?
9. Facilitator: Yes. So if I was nervous about going to the dentist and terrified of, say, going to war, but went ahead with both, then I'd be showing greater courage in going off to war – wouldn't I?
10. Jahred: I think using the word 'courage' is a bit strong if you're just nervous about going to the dentist.
11. Kian: What would you call it then?
12. Jahred: Well I'm not sure. I need to think about it. 'Nervousness' I suppose.

13. Lauryn: Well I did a bit of research before the session –
14. Faisal: You're always doing research!
15. Lauryn: And I found out that the word courage comes from the Latin word for 'heart' and also Middle French words for 'temper' and 'innermost feelings'. So if you're being courageous, I wonder if you're doing something despite your innermost feeling, or deep feeling, of being really scared. Or doing something, like fighting for your country, because you have such a strong feeling of love for it.
16. Jahred: Using that idea, I wouldn't say that just being nervous is an innermost feeling. I mean, it's not a deeply held feeling but more like a feeling that's on the surface.
17. Kian: So if you're in a really bad temper, which I think is an innermost feeling – like being in a blind rage where you're not thinking things through and feel enraged rather than frightened – and you go ahead and do something dangerous, is that being courageous?
18. Lauryn: Being in a rage means you've *lost* your temper. I found out that 'to temper' something means to moderate it.
19. Eve: I don't understand that.
20. Lauryn: I think it means 'to be moderate' about something and not extreme.
21. Facilitator: So as an example, a judge might temper a punishment with mercy – to moderate a prison sentence because of the particular circumstances of the crime.
22. Faisal: Like a crime of passion?
23. Facilitator: That's a useful example I think.
24. Hailey: Going back to Kian's point, if you do something dangerous without thinking and without feeling frightened – because you're so angry – then I don't think you're being courageous. You've just lost control of yourself. And another thought I've had is that innermost feelings are ones that you think about a lot – like the love for your country that Lauryn mentioned. When you're in a blind rage, like I said, you're not really thinking, but just reacting.
25. Jahred: So are you saying that to be courageous you've got to know what you're doing *and* be in control of your feelings of fear?

26. Hailey: Yes, that's what I'm saying. Although, I've had another thought ... When you fall in love with someone, are you in control of how you feel then? You know about the feeling of course and you're thinking about it, but you can't help yourself feeling that way.
27. Faisal: But you can still make choices and decisions about how you act in the relationship. In that sense you have control. But we haven't solved the problem of fearlessness being a synonym for courage, according to some dictionaries.
28. Lauryn: I don't think they do mean the same thing. I agree with Hailey that courage means doing something despite your fear. So, for example, if I was trapped in a burning building and Superman flew in to save me, then he's not being courageous because nothing can hurt him. But if an ordinary man risked his life to save me, I think he's being very courageous.
29. Eve: So are you saying that courage involves risk in every case?
30. Lauryn: Yes, but not necessarily risking your life. My auntie and uncle put their whole life savings into starting up a new business. I think they were courageous to do that.
31. Kian: But if a gambler bet his whole life savings on a horse race, then he wouldn't be courageous for risking all his money would he? I think he'd just be stupid.
32. Facilitator: If he was what you'd call a compulsive gambler – if he couldn't help himself – then maybe we wouldn't call his actions stupid.
33. Kian: No, maybe not. But he could try to get help though, from Gamblers' Anonymous or whatever.
34. Eve: But if he wasn't a compulsive gambler – if he just liked the thrill of risking his money – then could we say that he was feeling the fear and doing it anyway? If so, then he was being courageous.
35. Lauryn: I don't think that 'liking the thrill' is the same as 'feeling the fear'.
36. Eve: But can't you like feeling frightened – being on a fast fairground ride, for instance?
37. Jahred: But you're pretty safe on a fairground ride. If you were a soldier on the front line then you wouldn't be safe.

38. Facilitator: So are we saying that courage involves danger to yourself?
39. Hailey: If that's the case then the gambler wouldn't personally be in danger, so he wouldn't be courageous in risking his money.
40. Lauryn: So what we're saying is that to be courageous you need to feel fear – but control it; you need to be risking yourself personally; and you need to be in a dangerous situation?
41. Faisal: What about a cat burglar who risks his life to climb the outside of a high building to steal a valuable diamond? He'd be frightened but in control, risking himself personally in a dangerous situation. So he'd be courageous.
42. Eve: Yes, but he's doing something bad.
43. Lauryn: So are you saying that you can only be courageous if you're doing something good?
44. Kian: This makes it very complicated because we also have to try and work out what 'good' means.
45. Jahred: What if there were two soldiers who were enemies, each risking their lives for what they believed to be a good cause and believing that the enemy's cause was evil – are they both being courageous in going to war?
46. Lauryn: I'd say they were both being courageous within their own beliefs.
47. Eve: But what if the cause of one of the soldiers said that killing innocent people was OK if it helped you to win the war – how could that cause possibly be good?
48. Jahred: If I *truly* believe I'm fighting for a good cause in a war situation then I'm being courageous.
49. Faisal: But you might truly believe something because you've been brainwashed. We're back to what Kian said about things getting complicated ….

Lauryn: Which is why doing philosophy is such fun!

Commentary on the dialogue
2. Faisal begins to unpack the abstract idea of courage.
3. Giving some thinking and researching time between choosing the core question and beginning the dialogue allows children to clarify their thoughts and gather facts and evidence. Note

also that Lauryn has the confidence to challenge the 'received wisdom' of a dictionary that courage is synonymous with fearlessness.
5. Hailey is making further distinctions, framing it as a question to invite her friends' opinions.
6. Kian is building on Hailey's point.
7. The facilitator is guiding with a light touch and not trying to steer or control the dialogue.
8. Eve wants clarification of the term.
10. Jahred is expressing his agreement with the facilitator.
15. Through her research, Lauryn is able to make creative connections between concepts that feature in the dialogue.
18. Lauryn is actively thinking about the definitions she's come across and reflecting on what the everyday expression 'losing your temper' means, thus challenging the view held by some that 'temper' is the same as 'anger'.
19. Eve has the confidence to say she doesn't understand.
24. Hailey offers a reasoned argument.
28. Lauryn offers an example (a thought experiment in this case) to test her view.
29. Eve questions a generalisation.
30. Lauryn builds on the idea of risk by giving an example.
31. Kian challenges Lauryn's view on risk.
35. Lauryn makes a useful distinction.
36. Eve tests Lauryn's view.
39. Hailey builds on the facilitator's comment about personal danger.
40. Lauryn summarises her understanding of the main points so far.
41. Faisal tests the provisional definition of courage with a reasonable example.
44. Kian makes the very relevant point that philosophy gets complicated. The educator Will Ord feels that 'if you're not struggling you're not learning, just rehearsing what you already know'.
46. Lauryn deepens the discussion by reintroducing the notion of the relative nature of courage, picking up on the facilitator's earlier comment about contexts.

Matthew Lipman (page xi) said that philosophy begins when we discuss the language we use to discuss the world. In that sense a philosophical enquiry is different from an interesting discussion: it is a search for understanding and truth; and, as Will Ord maintains, with a sense of investigation at play. Behind the language are the concepts by which we understand the world. And out of those concepts, when examined carefully, thoroughly and rationality through philosophy, arise our values and beliefs, which we are increasingly able to modify and refine if we wish.

AFTERWORD

In 2011 at the Google Zeitgeist Conference in Hertfordshire the renowned physicist Stephen Hawking declared that 'Philosophy is dead'[20] on the grounds that basic questions about the nature of the universe could not be resolved without 'hard data' from space research and work being done; for example, at the Large Hadron Collider in Switzerland. On first hearing this I was reminded of something a teacher friend once said to me: 'In education the most valuable things can't be measured, while what we measure are not the most valuable things.' In that sense one can argue that philosophy doesn't generate 'hard data' in the form of benchmark measurements, but that in itself is no reason to deny or dismiss its value.

Professor Hawking's philosophy that 'philosophy is dead' raises a further insight, which is that science and philosophy explore the universe in different ways. Both are concerned with the fundamental nature of knowledge, reality and existence, but philosophy endeavours to explore these primarily through the medium of language and how that relates to our subjective experience of life, striving to penetrate further into ideas that may be mysterious and in some cases unanswerable, but that are not in any way 'imponderable' (Ricard and Trinh's *The Quantum and the Lotus* offers a clear example of how science and philosophy differ and yet how they are united in the aim of deepening our understanding of the universe).

Aside from that, teaching children to think philosophically cultivates an attitude and gives practice in a range of thinking skills that are of practical value in their learning and in the way they can conduct their lives. P4C helps children to become active seekers after wisdom by following a teacher's advice to 'Question everything!' – to which one philosophically literate pupil once replied, 'Why?'

Notes

1. www.sapere.org.uk/
2. www.philosophy-foundation.org
3. www.philosophyforschools.co.uk
4. http://webarchive.nationalarchives.gov.uk/20130401151715/www.education.gov.uk/publications/eOrderingDownload/QCA-04-1374.pdf
5. http://webarchive.nationalarchives.gov.uk/20110223175304/http://curriculum.qcda.gov.uk/key-stages-3-and-4/skills/personal-learning-and-thinking-skills/index.aspx
6. www.functionalskills.com/Functional-Skills/Functional-Skills-for-schools.php
7. www.livescience.com/33179-does-human-body-replace-cells-seven-years.html
8. http://coolcosmos.ipac.caltech.edu
9. www.philosophynews.com/post/2015/01/29/What-is-Truth.aspx
10. http://cw.routledge.com/textbooks/alevelphilosophy/data/AS/KnowledgeoftheExternalWorld/Secondaryqualities.pdf
11. http://steve-patterson.com/resolving-the-liars-paradox/
12. www.edutopia.org/blog/creating-emotionally-healthy-classroom-environment-mark-phillips
13. www.psychologytoday.com/blog/unique-everybody-else/201311/the-illusory-theory-multiple-intelligences
14. www.bbc.co.uk/news/business-39142030
15. www.theguardian.com/film/filmblog/2015/jul/27/inside-out-philosophical-mind-pixar-philosophy
16. http://philosophy.hku.hk/think/phil/101q.php
17. https://philosophytalk.org/blog/why-there-something-rather-nothing
18. www.space.com/32728-parallel-universes.html
19. http://greatergood.berkeley.edu/article/item/when_courage_goes_bad
20. www.telegraph.co.uk/technology/google/8520033/Stephen-Hawking-tells-Google-philosophy-is-dead.html

References

Abbott, I. and Ryan, T. *The Unfinished Revolution*. Stafford: Network Educational Press, 2000. See also www.21learn.org/

Baggini, J. *Do They Think You're Stupid? (100 Ways of Spotting Spin and Nonsense from the Media, Pundits and Politicians*. London: Granta Books, 2008.

Blackburn, S. *The Big Questions: Philosophy*. London: Quercus, 2009.

Bowkett, S. *Countdown to Creative Writing*. Abingdon, Oxon: Routledge, 2009.

Bowkett, S. *Jumpstart! Thinking Skills and Problem Solving*. Abingdon, Oxon: Routledge, 2015.

Bowkett, S. and Hogston, K. *Jumpstart! Wellbeing*. Abingdon, Oxon: Routledge, 2017.

Buckley, J. *Pocket P4C: Getting Started with Philosophy for Children*. Chelmsford, Essex: One Slice Press, 2011.

Campbell, J. *The Power of Myth*. New York: Doubleday, 1991.

Campbell, J. *The Way of Myth*. Boston, MA: Shambala, 1994.

Cohen, M. *101 Ethical Dilemmas*. London: Routledge, 2003.

Cowley. S. *Getting the Buggers to Behave*. London: Continuum, 2006.

Egan, K. *The Educated Mind: How Cognitive Tools Shape our Understanding*. Chicago, IL: University of Chicago Press, 1997.

Engel, S.M. *Fallacies and Pitfalls of Language: The Language Trap*. New York: Dover Publications, 1994.

Irwin. W., Brown, R. and Decker, K.S. *Terminator and Philosophy: I'll be Back, Therefore I Am* (The Blackwell Philosophy and Pop Culture Series). Oxford: Blackwell, 2009.

Joseph, J. *Should I Flush My Goldfish Down the Loo? And Other Modern Morals*. London: Hodder & Stoughton, 2007.

LaBossiere, M. *What Don't You Know?* London: Continuum, 2008.

Law, S. *The Philosophy Files/The Philosophy Files 2*. London: Orion, 2000/2003.

References

Morgan, N. and Saxton, J. *Asking Better Questions*. Markam, Ont.: Pembroke, 1994.

Percival, S. *The Practical Guide to Revision Techniques*. Stafford: Network Educational Press, 2005.

Pohl, F. and Kornbluth, C. *The Space Merchants*. London: Gollancz, 2003.

Polkinghorne, J. *Exploring Reality: The Intertwining of Science and Religion*. New Haven, CT, and London: Yale University Press/SPCK, 2005.

Postman, N. and Weingartner, C. *Teaching as a Subversive Activity*. Harmondsworth, Middlesex: Penguin, 1971.

Reps, P. *Zen Flesh, Zen Bones*. Harmondsworth, Middlesex: Pelican, 1980.

Ricard, M. and Trinh, X.T. *The Quantum and the Lotus*. New York: Three Rivers Press, 2001.

Rowlands, M. *The Philosopher at the End of the Universe*. London: Ebury Press, 2005.

Scruton, R. *An Intelligent Person's Guide To Philosophy*. London: Penguin, 1999.

Stanley, S. with Bowkett, S. *But Why? Developing Philosophical Thinking in the Classroom*. Stafford: Network Educational Press, 2004. See also http://sarastanley.co.uk/

Stephen, A. *Why We Think the Things We Think: Philosophy in a Nutshell*. London: Michael O'Mara Books, 2017.

Stock, G. *The Kids' Book of Questions*. New York: Workman Publishing, 2004.

Sutcliffe, R. and Williams, S. *The Philosophy Club: An Adventure in Thinking*. Newport, Pembrokeshire: Dialogue Works, 2000.

Truss, L. *Eats, Shoots and Leaves: The Zero Tolerance Approach to Punctuation*. London: Profile Books, 2003.

Von Oech, R. *A Whack on the Side of the Head: How You Can Be More Creative*. London: HarperCollins, 1990.

Warburton, N. *Philosophy – The Basics*. London: Routledge, 2004.